Experiences
of Physical Phenomena
in the 21st Century.

by

Ann E. Harrison

—

Published by
Saturday Night Press Publications
England.
www.snppbooks.com
snppbooks@gmail.com

ISBN 978-1-908421-60-9

www.snppbooks.com

Cover design by Ann Harrison - Saturday Night Press Publications.
Art work from "Starshine" – a water-colour crayon sketch by Tom Harrison.

Dedication

to all our friends and companions in both worlds,
who have assisted me in bringing this book into being,
in the hope of helping those who read it to realize
what is possible when there is dedication
of purpose and love.

Acknowledgements

My profound thanks go to all these mediums and their 'sitters', for giving years of your lives to help those in Spirit have the opportunity to connect through you, and to make us aware that ~ There is no separation and we can connect across the veil of 'Death'.

My thanks go especially to:

~ Stewart Alexander for allowing me to quote extensively from the recordings made over 20 years sitting with him and the circle.

~ Robert and Barbara McLernon for permission to use the material relating to their wonderful Acacia Centre and the contact we had with spirit folks through his mediumship.

~ My friends in West Yorkshire, to use the transcripts you gave us. Such valuable detail, although who could ever forget those special evenings and the phenomena we experienced.

~ Katie Halliwell for permission to include the drawings she did for her books 'Experiences of Trance, Physical Mediumship and Associated Phenomena with the Stewart Alexander Circle'(Pt1-3) and the excerpt from her new book 'Touching the Next Horizon'.

CONTENTS

Key:

The main names in the recording transcripts of the Stewart Alexander Circle, and their background or relationships.

The Spirit team

White Feather. opens and closes the sittings, speaks briefly

Walter Stinson. brother and main control of Mina Crandon (Margery), now in charge of the 'Proceedings' at Stewart's circle.

Vanguard – later known as Dr. Barnett. / Also for unidentified spirit visitor.

Dr Barnett. the communicator through George Valiantine in the 1920s (see Denis Bradley books)

Freda (Johnson). helps loved ones communicate with sitters.

Christopher – the cheeky, ice breaker, speaks child-like.

Circle members and Frequent Visitors

Stewart Alexander, –the medium).

Ray Lister, – circle leader.

June Lister, – Ray's wife.

Denise, – Ray and June's daughter.

Gaynor, – Stewart's sister. (passed in 2009)

Michael, – Stewart's brother.

Peter, – circle member in 1990s

Janet, – circle member in 1990s

Lindsey, – Gaynor's daughter. (only present once, emigrated)

Lisa, – Gaynor's other daughter, circle member

Carol, – circle member .

Katie Halliwell, – honorary member.

Tom, – Harrison, circle member in 1990s & later hon. member.
                    (in spirit after Oct 2010)

Ann, – Tom's wife, circle member in 1990s & later hon. member.

Chris, – circle member – not shortened.

Jane, – circle member – not shortened to avoid confusion.

Jackie Boyd, (shortened to Jk. in conversations) a visitor.

Introduction

In 1990, three weeks after Norman, my first husband, died he returned through an unknown medium to a friend of his sister at a Spiritualist Church sixty miles away. When Bess told me I could not wait to know more and make my own contact. Within two months I had contact and my journey began. I was accepted into the little church in Hull and six months later I began a course of study with Mavis Pitilla at the Arthur Findlay College. Clairvoyance and clairsentience developed and I began also to write poetry that streamed through when I had meditated, usually to be used as readings for church services .

When in September 1993 a friend persuaded me to go for a weekend stay at a local Spiritual Centre, where there was to be a talk about Physical Mediumship, I had no idea how my life would change and how physically close spirit could draw.

Tom Harrison spoke that day about the wonders he had witnessed through the mediumship of his mother, Minnie Harrison, in their Home Circle in Middlesbrough in the 1940s and 50s. He had recorded vital episodes in his small book *Visits by Our Friends from the Other Side*" but he was by then 75 years-old and had largely stopped travelling to tell people of his experiences. He found travelling long distances alone was very tiring. He'd been the first manager at the Arthur Findlay College when it opened in 1966, and I persuaded him to go back to the College on "Experimental Week" a few weeks later where he was able to give his talk again.

After the talk at that week offers poured in for him to travel to tell their people in their churches and centres of his experiences. Some were in Scotland and he said "I don't know. It is a long way..." At that time he was living in the south of England so I said "I'll be your driver. I'll help set up." The following Easter we went on the long journey to Scotland, giving three talks (Edinburgh, Arbroath and Glasgow) in the four days. We never stopped travelling for the next six years! and we were married in 1998 – but that's a different story.

Because of the Noah's Ark Society Tom had got to know Stewart Alexander and he was invited to sit in Stewart's Home Circle whenever he was in the North. In January '94 he got permission to take me to my first ever Physical Mediumship séance. That was my introduction to the wonderful world of tangible, physical spirit contact which has continued until this day.

Over the last 29 years I have sat with five physical mediums who demonstrate to larger groups beyond their home (development) circles, at least four other physical mediums in private home circles – one of them being our own home circle. I have witnessed communications – both philosophical and evidential – through at least seven more 'good' trance mediums. Amongst these latter I have not included the mediums from the first two 'physical' groups, as a state of trance is usually essential for the phenomena to take place – but not always.

Leslie Flint the reknowned Direct Voice medium of the 1950-90s is recorded joining in the conversations with the spirit communicating by independent voice. Mrs Perriman in the 1930s was reported as not being in trance during several direct voice sessions. In large group demonstations the spirit team have been known to bring Stewart Alexander out of trance so that he can speak from the cabinet while the trumpet is at a distance from him somewhere across the room. This is so that any sceptical sitters can know he is not out of his chair and waving the trumpet about – as has been alleged to be so with many mediums across the decades.

However, a deep state of trance is usual for the phenomena to take place. So I invite you to sit back and enjoy my experiences with these amazing dedicated people who give so much of their time for those in spirit to be able to link from the World Beyond in ways that show how close they can be when we give them the opportunity.

Forms of Physical Phenomena

Physical Mediumship is when something – not instigated physically by the medium or one of the sitters – happens in a room that everyone can see or hear or feel. Spirit people are not just working inside the mind of the medium, as with clairvoyance etc. — but out there, hopefully in light, but very often because of the low levels energy that is available, and the sensitivity of the substances that they work with, they still have to work mainly in the dark.

To achieve this you need a 'sensitive' who has usually been able to develop a state of trance – like a deep sleep. A state of 'unconsciousness' that the spirit team can work with to produce what we call psychic or physical phenomena. Trance, in itself, is a wonderful state to achieve, deep or not so deep – as long as you can get yourself out of the way to allow any face changes and words to be seen or expressed. Then, hopefully, as the development of the medium grows, the spirit team which has developed around the medium can show how they are able to influence this earthly state of ours.

When a group of people sit together in harmony, with an intent to communicate with loved ones who have gone before, then maybe amazing, seemingly impossible things, will happen. Many different types of phenomena can take place within a physical mediumship circle.

Firstly, there is the feeling of love that is felt when the spirit essence is present and to feel that 'energy – the 'force' of an 'invisible' materialisation – to feel it standing in front of you – to feel the energy coming from it is quite amazing. They are able to manipulate energy in our world in ways that is at times impossible to understand. As one new sitter said, at the end of his first séance in a circle in Spain, he had felt 'very nervous before we started but once it had started the energy that built up made you feel that you couldn't be frightened of anything.'

Physical objects can appear and disappear – without physical contact – **Apports** – a small coin, a "new home" card, a fridge magnet can be in the room at the end of the séance, or something might have been taken out and be found elsewhere in the house, though all doors and window were closed.

In the phenomenon known as **Telekinesis** objects can be picked up and moved around the room– like the crinoline lady bell pictured here. This was used in the Minnie Harrison circle in the 1940-50s and in our circle in the '90s.

Imagine the feeling when an invisible 'arm' in the darkness is waving it about over your head. It weighs 1½ pounds and it is very scary. I have had it happen. They used to ring it in our home circle when we lived near Selby and to have that over your head and think 'What's holding it up?' – I know there's a psychic rod – gulp

Crinoline lady bell.

'Yes!' Other things, drumsticks are drummed, discarded jumpers, even chairs, have been moved even tossed around the room – all sorts of things can happen.

A conical instrument known as a '**trumpet**' may move around the room, whirling or dancing. This usually is marked by tiny pieces of luminous tape or paint so that you know where it is and what it is doing. Spirit folk may tap you with the 'trumpet' as it moves around the room. People think it is really just to have a great lot of fun with it and argue whether or not the medium is standing up and waving it about – this is why mediums like to be fastened down so that sitters know they can't be moving around. Sometimes the trumpet is taken up to the ceiling (way out of a medium's reach.)

In Tom's circle, if the spirit team couldn't manifest a voice, they devised a way of giving signals, so up and down would show that one spirit person was there, another might go sideways, and Sunrise, the circle guide, always moved the trumpet round in a circle like the sun. One night in the 1940s, somebody said "He always goes the same way." The trumpet stopped dead and went round the other way!

And ever since then, in Stewart's circle, in our own home circle and elsewhere we would see it. Sunrise was showing that he is there . He always goes both ways and we can say "Hello Sunrise it's lovely to have you with us."

Its main purpose is to transmit a voice away from the medium and close to a recipient. The trumpet is at all times connected to the medium by ectoplasmic rods or rather in this case 'tubes'. This is known as **Direct Voice.** If the voice is extremely quiet they use the 'trumpet'. A very quiet voice may go in and a louder voice would be heard at the other end. Tom told us in their circle, if someone was hard of hearing the trumpet would go right up against their

Infra red photo of Minnie Harrison and the ectoplasmic support of the trumpet.

good ear, the little voice would be amplified and they would hear it.

In a circle where the phenomenon has developed sufficiently well voices may be heard coming directly out of the air well away from the medium – and is known as **'Independent Direct Voice'.** This is when the spirit team has been able to construct a 'voice box' by the means of ectoplasmic energy withdrawn from the medium (and sitters) through which the spirits can project their voices at some distance, even moving it around while continuing to speak.

Spirit writing may appear on paper, only to be read later when the light is put on. This one was written one night in our Home circle when we had a visitor sitting for the first time. The notepad had been closed by spirit and this was written on the back cover.

Spirit lights like small torch beams may appear and disappear in the darkness. Tom said in their circle they asked what they were and they were told it's 'the lit end of an ectoplasm rod' – a little bit like fibre-optics today. The end just glows but you don't see the rest of it. These lights can appear all over the room, sometimes in different colours.

In **Transfiguration** the medium's face appears to change shape and develop different features or a mask effect appears in front of the medium's face building to show a recognisable face.

The ultimate of course in physical mediumship is – **Materialisation** – solid forms of family and friends returning from the dead with their own personalities, with their love and sometimes with their voices– (referred to as 'spirit people'), but just as they were and wanting to be recognised.

How wonderful to be able to see it, in full, in light. It must be mind-blowing. I've not witnessed that. I've felt the energy of forms standing in front of me —solid in the dark. I've been touched and had my hand held by Tom, solid in the darkness. I've seen parts of bodies, hands, arms, and a shadowy head and shoulder in red light but never a full form. We simply haven't had enough energy to be able to do it even though the medium Stewart Alexander has sat for many, many years. With Kai Muegge I have seen the profile of a face briefly in white light. A lot depends on the available energy – of the medium's health / strength and our preparedness to sit. I remember reading of a group in South Wales sitting for two weeks to prepare for their sitting with Alec Harris – and a very special night they had.

There is also a very specialised form of phenomena demanding great sensitivity and that is Matter thru' matter. This is where solid earthly objects are able to pass through other "solid" earthly objects. More on this later.

But if you haven't a medium who has developed to these levels why not start with a table as we did in a circle in West Yorkshire, though maybe not as large, and/or a Ouija board and a great deal of dedication and patience.

Always remember, if you do start to sit, you ask for protection and guidance from the best that can be reached, and sit with honesty and the highest intent to communicate, to help.

My First Sittings in a Circle

As already mentioned in the Introduction, Tom had got to know Stewart through the Noah's Ark Society in the early days of its foundation and had been invited to sit in Stewart's circle whenever he was in the North. Eventually at the beginning of '94 he got permission for me to sit also.

I was invited to sit, just the one time, and that night I was greeted with:

"White Feather knows much about you. White Feather would like to reassure his little sister that there is nothing whatsoever to fear. We come only in love to be of service. For a short time, we shall remove the barrier between our two worlds to that we can commune together as old friends."

That evening my dad, who'd passed just six weeks after my husband, tried to speak through the trumpet and then Christopher (Stewart's 'child' control) passed on a message from my husband talking about 'apples – apples'. We had planted about a dozen apple trees in our garden so he was very concerned, as he had been the one to prune them and tie them into shape along the espalier wires. Something I had been neglecting to do.

At that stage Tom was just visiting from his home in the south, coming to me when we had to travel to do a talk, so Tom was able to sit about once a month in that first year. Fortunately for me, Ray, the circle leader, and Stewart agreed that I should sit with them again whenever Tom returned.

On this second occasion Walter asked Denise (the daughter of the family in whose home we sat) if she would like to feel his hand and that I could as well. Or should I say the spirit team had decided it and Walter voiced the invitation.

Walter Stinson was the brother of 'Margery the Medium'– Mina Crandon, and had been Mina's guide in the 1920s. He was the one that did the amazing experiments. If you ever get a chance to read the book *Margery the Medium* and read about some of the experiments that took place, they are just mind-blowing; the way she was fastened up, chained-up, manacled in a box so she couldn't move at all and still things happened — physical things happened out in the room. And they still claimed she was a fraud!

Stewart developed an interest in her work and started to write about her. In spirit, Walter determined to find out who this man was who was championing his sister. Eventually he decided to work with him. He is in charge of the phenomena that takes place. He doesn't look back to the things they did all those years ago, he just wants to move forward.

For some reason Spirit seemed to have quickly taken a liking to me – particularly Walter, and that evening, one at a time, we had to change places with June (Ray's wife) who sat to the right of Stewart. When it was my turn I was instructed to put my left hand out on to Stewart's right hand, which was resting on the arm of the chair with a rope fastening his arm to the chair. A large hand was placed on the top of mine. I was amazed at how soft it was – it was large – totally unlike Stewart's hand – but it was so soft, so gentle – and he then tapped the back of my hand. You could hear the taps. It was solid. It wasn't just airy-fairy stuff that could make no sound. You could feel and hear the tapping – flesh on flesh.

Before the phenomena had started that evening Walter had answered one of Michael's questions which I feel is pertinent to the experiment he had just carried out and what was to come later.

Walter. Michael, you will recall, I think, that you asked about Ectoplasm. You asked why it is that it has been on occasions, in the past, that the materialised heads – I think you said – tended to be either smaller or larger than what is normal.

Michael. That's right

Walter. Okay. I think I said we would discuss this on another occasion. (*Michael.* Yes, you did.) That occasion is now. I am beginning now to take adequate control of the medium so that I can concentrate on what I am saying rather than what I am doing. You understand? (*Michael.* Yes, excellent.) ... Good – let me just say this – I said to you that sometimes the materialised heads may be the size, let us say, of an egg or could be the size of twice that of a football. (*Michael.* Yes) Okay. Now that may seem awfully strange to you, because you would rightly question why if it is in reality a human being that is materialising from my side of life, why the size should not always be as you would expect it to be. Now let me tell you that when we, at this stage of development, withdraw the energy which you refer to as Ectoplasm from this medium, then what we are actually trying to do is not to clothe ourselves in that energy, in that Ectoplasm. What we are trying to do is to impress ourselves, our thoughts.

Michael. So it is a mental process?

Walter. It is indeed so, when Christopher said that he was trying to show himself, he was not trying to imply that he himself was coated in Ectoplasm, but that he was impressing his thoughts within the Ectoplasm which then reacts can be moulded by those souls. Okay. You understand? Michael, you understand?

Michael. I'm very slow at understanding Walter. No I do understand what you are saying, but I'm trying to imagine what the process must be like – very complex.

Walter. Yes Ectoplasm is extremely sensitive, extremely sensitive – you know from what you have been told and from what you have read in the past, that in many respects there are many dangers involved in the externalisation of Ectoplasm. (*Michael.* Yes.) You know that if a light of any kind is suddenly introduced when it is unexpected, then that Ectoplasm can be adversely affected by the light such that it immediately returns to the body of the medium. It is an ultra-sensitive substance that comes from the human body, but it is contained within all human bodies. What I am actually trying to say is that the chemists from this side of life withdraw the Ectoplasm from the medium, but at that stage it is in a very unorganised form. Now Christopher would then press his thoughts, and his thoughts would then mould the Ectoplasm.

Michael. So he would be thinking how he wanted to show himself.

Walter. Of his appearance – Yes, yes.

16

Michael. But that would open another can of worms, doesn't it Walter. What would happen, Walter, if he thought of himself as somebody else?

Walter. Then what would happen would be that you would then perceive his thought – you would then see exactly what he was thinking.

Michael. The person he was imitating?

Walter. Exactly, exactly so you are not actually seeing him as such – but his thoughts.

Michael. Therefore you have to be very careful because it could be an entity purporting to be somebody else.

Walter. Oh, indeed it could but of course in a circle of this kind where we have such contact with you, and we work with you week by week then there is every protection surrounding you whenever you sit. Okay. It is really only in a circle which has not yet attained that level of contact with our world where there are possibilities of dangers and problems such as you describe. (*Michael.* Yes, that's fascinating.) So therefore, in that way, within that ectoplasm, a hundred faces could materialise at the same time and you could find yourself looking upon a mass of Ectoplasm in which was contained 100 heads. But that would only be the thought of someone over here – one of the operators.[1]

Michael. It's a very difficult job isn't it, Walter. First of all, remembering what he used to look like and then to show himself at the right size.

Walter. Yes exactly. (*Michael.* Very difficult.) and that is precisely why sometimes these heads can be exceedingly small, much smaller than normal and on other occasions much greater in size than what is normal. Okay, Ann do you understand all this?

Ann. Yes, yes, I do Walter.

Walter. Well I'm baffled myself.

Ann. If you are thinking of being happy inside yourself and that expression you put on to your own face in this world; if you want to show a frown even though you are not feeling like a frown or feeling angry, you can put that expression on your face...

---

1. As was seen in the Cenotaph photographs taken by Ada Deane in the 1920s

Walter. Yes, yes very similar, very similar. You see if you wish to paint a picture then you have to acquire the materials – you have to pick up the paint brush and then you begin physically to draw that picture, but what you are putting on to that paper or canvas is the thought that is within your mind. You are transferring your thought on to the paper or onto the canvas. What we are talking about, or spirit are, is through thought transferring what is within his mind directly onto or into the Ectoplasm which reacts and is moulded by those thoughts. There is a very strong simile here. Okay.

Michael. So is it a similar system for independent voice Walter?

Walter. No. no. We shall speak of this later. But I wanted you to understand. (*All.* Yes, thank you). This is important because of the development which we hope will take place over the next few weeks. Well, I hope that that has been an adequate explanation.

In my records of that evening it says:

Following the holding of Denise's and my hands – the team went on that evening to produce the outflow of ectoplasm from Stewart and in brief exposure to red light we were able to see it at the side of Stewart's face with sitters saying there was more than previous week.

Following this the cabinet curtains were partly closed and Walter asked Gaynor to pick up the luminous plaque from the floor and place it on the table luminous side up.

Walter. Would you like to see the hand of a man who has been dead for 80 years?

To raise the vibrations Ray played the music and we sang along. Within a few minutes we saw some fingers holding up the plaque and we saw Walter's hand – a big hand against the luminous surface. As Michael said it was 'the right size' to his thinking. (And I've always experienced it as a big hand.)

Walter. It just goes to show what can be done when people gather together in love and harmony with dedication. What I was able to do there was not a thought projection within the Ectoplasm. That was a coating of ectoplasm around my Etheric body. Ann, what do you think?

Ann. I think it is wonderful. Having heard Tom talk about it I didn't expect to see anything like this. I'm speechless.

Music was played loudly and after taps, the trumpets rose and danced about as we sang along. Sunrise made his sign with Tom's trumpet, and it pushed Tom in the chest as a greeting.

Later Christopher signed off, and telling us we had to come again. As he said "Bye, bye." another voice took control of Stewart. It was Norman, he struggled to say "I just want to speak with Ann ... Ann..." Then he tried something to say something like peas –please–pre... and after struggling managed to say pleased added "Ann, Ann, all I want to do is to tell you how much I love you."

Ann. I know you do.

He struggled to form the words, while all were encouraging him. Finally he managed to say "The trees, the trees, how are the trees?"

Ann. "The apple trees?"

Norman. Yes.

Ann. "One or two are not doing well but the others are very good. I need to do some pruning on them I think."

We then heard the sound of kisses blown and "I'm alright now. Sorry I can't talk."

Gaynor. You've done well.

Tom. That was tremendous!

Ray. For the first time too, by-gum!

White Feather then closed the evening.

Here I have to add that although I couldn't say that Norman's voice was identifiable it was certainly very different from Stewart's own voice and from that of Walter with its Canadian influence and Christopher's child-like pitch.

I had forgotten at the time when he was talking about the trees was that I'd actually fed them with his ashes. As one medium said to me "He is saying, 'I made good fertiliser.' "

They know what you are up to!

An Informative Evening

On the next occasion we were able to sit with the circle it was more an evening for a chat with Walter, with him passing on information – while the spirit team, we were sure, were working in the background. Tom had told me, in their circle they were told there was a team of twenty scientists planning, building and trying to perfect the phenomena before moving ahead. It seems this was one of those evenings, and a perfect opportunity for Stewart's brother to have more of his questions answered.

Walter began this part of the evening by asking after my well-being: – "Ann, how are you,"

Ann. Very well thank you, Walter.

Michael. I'm sure she felt better after being stroked by the hand of a man who has been dead for 80 years!

Walter. Well, if Ann felt better because of that, I had a tremendous thrill myself. (*laughter*) ...Yes– it's an awful long time since I was able to touch a lady on your side of life – and I'm still a man. Okay Michael – think up your questions. I can always rely upon his enquiring mind placing the most darned awkward questions. Okay.

Michael. Tell us about yourself Walter.

Walter. Would you like me to tell you something about Walter Stinson? (*Michael.* Yes.) That should be interesting – as long as no–one feels that would be boring. (*Michael.* Not at all). Okay. You know that I passed away into this world many years ago. Of course, I had no knowledge of an after–life at all. Indeed, I hadn't given the matter any thought whatsoever – because I was a young man in my prime – as you say – so imagine my shock when I found myself out of the body and in this world. For a time, I couldn't accept that I had passed beyond the veil.

Michael. That was an accident, wasn't it, Walter?

Walter. Indeed it was. Yes. But we shall not go into that. That is, as you will understand somewhat painful, even now, for me to recall. (*Michael.* Sure). One thing I was to discover very quickly, and that was that I, together with all in this world, were able from time to time to be able to look down upon your world – to see those people whom we had left behind and whom we had loved – and still love. And it was in that way that my Sis, who in life had been so very close to me, how I went into her home and saw that she was beginning to try and develop mediumship. And you can understand why it was that I was so keen, so enthusiastic in wanting to work with her to do what I could – from my side of life. So, in a way we were still together, we were still as one working together as we had done upon the earth plane. (*Michael.* Yes, right). Of course, in those early days while she was still developing her gift, none of us, either on her side of life or on this side of life realised what lay ahead. I am talking, referring there to all the heartache. If of course we had known, we would not have followed that particular path. I would have advised her against it – but of course, once we had set foot upon that path, once we had started down that road, there was no turning back. We had to keep going.

It then became a question of proving at all costs the reality of my world – to prove at all costs that Walter Stinson had survived the grave. You understand? (*Michael.* Oh yes – certainly.) Yes – and then the rest, as you say, is history. You know what happened – what transpired – you know, Margery, as she was known in your world, could have become a priceless possession of the Spiritualist movement. Instead, she became something of a curiosity in the so-called world of Psychical Research. ...

But we have to look ahead –what matters now is the future and not the past. I do this and I return to your Circle with the blessing of my Sis. (*Michael.* Oh, good, good.) But as you know, this time we shall do things rather differently.

Michael. We've talked before about Ectoplasm and how you clothe your bodies – tell us about your bodies.

Walter. You ask about my body – my body is much the same as your body. I have arms and feet and legs, I have head, arms, hands – everything you have, I have.

Michael. Right – but do you have a heart and a circulation?

Walter. Yes – I have everything that you have. But it is vibrating at a different rate to that of your own.

Michael. Yes – but it feels solid to you as ours feels solid to us.

Walter. Yes – indeed.

Michael. ....because you are all vibrating at the same level?

Walter. Yes – exactly. (*Michael.* That's interesting) My world is the world of reality – yours is the world of illusion! No doubt you've heard it referred to before. (*Michael.* Yes) Everything that you have you also has an Etheric equivalent. When you pass from your world into this, then you leave behind that portion of yourself which belongs to your world which vibrates at the same rate. But in this world, you have the eternal body. Your brain, your physical brain, is merely a tool of your mind. Your mind is the real you, the eternal you.

Michael. So do you have a brain, Walter?

Walter. No – a Mind. I have the spiritual equivalent to the brain which is the Mind. The brain is nothing but a tool of the mind. Do I explain that to your satisfaction?

Michael. Does the body grow on your side, Walter, like when a child passes?

Walter. Yes, in that case it continues to grow until it reaches maturity – until it is fully developed. (*Michael.* But it doesn't go past that?) No, because there is no such thing as decay in this world of mind – there is no such thing as ageing in this world of mind.

Michael. Right. Do you have other similar things as here – do you see grass and trees?

Walter. Yes indeed our world is a real world and everything within this world of Mind is as real to us as what everything in your world is to you.

Michael. So you have seas, land, weather?

Walter. Yes. Now you want to ask I suppose about the seasons in my world. (*Michael.* Yes) You want to ask where the rain comes from (*Michael.* Yes – it follows on, doesn't it?) Yes, and if you ask me at our next sitting, I'll be pleased to go into that. Don't forget.

Michael. No. – Can I ask one final little question – because of the nature of Ectoplasm itself – whether there is some way artificially that we can help the medium? (*Walter.* No.) I've heard about things being brought into the séance room – Ectoplasm must comprise of something chemically. Can you produce in your laboratory a tree, a blade of grass, a flower – can you produce a heart, a mind, or something that is capable of love and expression? Can you produce something with emotion?

Walter. Ectoplasm as you refer to it is a real substance a living substance within each and every one of you. It is neither physical nor is it spiritual – it is the only substance – the only energy that exists which is between the two states. You understand?

Michael. But it is a living substance?

Walter. It is a living substance – it is a part of our medium as we take it from his body. If we were to not return that to him, then he would possibly haemorrhage. It would create enormous problems in terms of his health and well–being – and here is the very reason why physical mediumship in the wrong hands can be destroyed – why it is dangerous to the health of the medium and to some extent that of the sitters.

Michael. That's right, this is why I was thinking in terms of helping it artificially, so that it wouldn't have the same danger.

Walter. Michael, if you are able to dream up a way in which this can be done then please tell us. After all it would be far simpler for us to do that, but at the moment I can tell you that there is no substitute at all for Ectoplasm not as far as I am aware. (*Michael.* Right.) ... Ann, is this all making good sense to you? (*Michael.* Yes – sorry Ann.) (*Ann.* Yes. – *laughter from all.*) Well Michael answers to anything. (*more laughter*) Well it is important to have an enquiring mind of course. (*Ann.* Yes) and we are always willing to answer sensible questions which are placed before us with sincerity.

Michael. I worry about Stewart, of course.

Walter. Well, let us do the worrying there.

At this point Gaynor, Stewart's sister (who sat to the left of Stewart) asked a question of Walter – "Walter – what happens to our bodies which are so old and possibly so ill when we pass over?"

Walter. Let me repeat what I just said Gaynor – and that is that your physical body is of the physical world with all its imperfections, with all its illnesses and aches and pains – that has no reflection whatsoever on the real body, the real mind the Spiritual body – that is perfection and will always be perfection. I want to be certain that you understand the nature of life in-so-far as it is within my capabilities to explain it to you. ... If you lose an arm now, you have merely lost your physical arm – not your spiritual arm ... I understand the question well, that is why you've heard people returning to your earth saying – I would not return to Earth for anything. I don't want to come back because the bodies in my world are perfection. They are freed from the limitations of the physical flesh.

This led on to Tom and Janet's questions:

Tom. What about those who became mentally ill and very depressed – They still need help on your side?

Walter. Oh yes Tom – yes – and for that reason we have many people over here who are anxious to help – we have hospitals, not in the way that you have hospitals, but really to treat the mind and help people because the mind IS the individual. Yes – the mind is all–important.

Janet. Can I just ask something?

Walter. June, you can ask me anything (*Janet.* It's Janet.) Oh yes (*Tom.* She's awake!) Yes, she needs to be awake, Tom.

Janet. ... Right Walter – elderly people who pass over are often seen by mediums as being much younger than when they passed over. Is it the body that is younger or just the mind?

Walter. It is both. The mind of course has the advantage that it has accumulated a great deal of experience and knowledge through its earthly life. That knowledge and those experiences can never be taken away from the individual. They are the person. Okay?

Walter then went on to describe my father and to pass on a message of love from him and this was followed by a further link with "the gentleman who brings so much love to you, so much love, – he gives his name as Norman – your husband. (*Ann.* That's right. It's lovely to know he's here.) Okay, I think he had quite a keen mind (*Ann.* Yes he did.) Did he come here with cancer? (*Ann.* Yes) Well he wants you to know that he has listened to what I have been saying and he can answer questions which Gaynor has asked – and to some extent which Janet has asked – and that is that his body now is perfection. (*Ann.* Good.) There's no pain whatsoever – all that belongs to your earth plane – has no part of this world. (*Ann.* Yes, I know that. – Does he still enjoy crosswords?) (*laughter.*) Well – funnily enough – as I am speaking to you now, he has a paper in his hand and a pen. (*much laughter*) Yes, indeed – but do you Ann? (*Ann.* Do crosswords?) Yes. (*Ann.* No.) No , but did he always ask you what this meant and that the answer to that was? (*Ann.* Yes.) Yes – but you found it all rather boring!" (*Ann.* No – too difficult usually.)

Another wonderful personal link.

After Walter had left us that evening it continued with the following interchange.

A man's deep voice, quite loud and clear. slowly and deliberately was heard: "I'm coming as fast as I am able. (that's very good ... you're.. welcome) it's not as simple as I had hoped. – (*Tom.* No it isn't – but it will get better.) I am perfectly all right, but at the moment I am having to concentrate so hard (*Peter.* Take our power friend.) I have it Peter – (*laughter) – (Peter.* You're welcome.) I have not spoken before in your Circle.

Ray. We didn't think we recognised your voice. You're going to tell us who you are then.

"I am indeed – my name is William Stead. (*Various voices.* Oh! William Stead! / Good evening. / *Ray.* 1912./ Ray is knowledgeable.)

Tom. That's right – Well this is very interesting.

Stead. It is very interesting for me also – (*Tom.* Good.) though rather frustrating because I am encountering such terrible difficulties (*Tom.* For the first time – exceptional) I am of course not without practice, only I have not spoken here – bear with me. (*Tom.* Certainly – you are doing very well – you've come to a loving circle.) I have come here because I had to take this opportunity to say 'Thank you' to Mr Harrison. (*Tom.* Oh! thank you.) You know that here in this world of ours there are a countless number of people who when upon your earth gave all for the cause (*Tom.* Yes.) There are not so many people in your world today who are doing that now – but you are one, sir. (*Tom.* Thank you very much.) I have a greeting to pass on to you from Mr Maurice Barbanell – (*Tom.* From Maurice Barbanell!) He always respected you – he wants you to know that he has been re–united with his great Love. *(Various voices.* Yes – good – lovely.) (*Tom.* It's overwhelming.) He will not forget from all on this side of life who were brothers and sisters in this cause. I thank you deeply Mr Harrison. (*Tom.* Thank you – I do what I can.) Your work is by no means finished. (*Tom.* I hope not.) You may be re–assured on that. (*Tom.* Thank you.) God bless you – God bless you."

Tom. God bless you – thank you for coming.

Within a minute another control spoke – rather hesitant and softly, everyone encouraged her. "Can you not hear me?" (*Various.* Yes we can hear you –you're doing well.)

Unfortunately, she was unable to say any more!

Walter immediately followed.

Walter. Well. Can you?! ... yes of course you can. (*laughter*) Okay. Well I hope this will not prove to be too much of a disappointment but there is very little that we can do this evening with physical manifestations – we have spoken together this evening like old friends (*All.* Yes, yes.) it is rather wonderful isn't it (*All.* Yes –we enjoyed it– what it's about, communication.) Okay Ann – Have you anything you would like to ask whilst I am still here?

Ann. Yes – I wanted to know how you came to work with Stewart – was it through his interest in your sister's work or were you interested in him before he became interested in your sister's work.

Walter. Well, I'll tell you. Over twenty years ago I had never even heard his name. I therefore had no interest whatsoever in him, what he was doing in his mediumship nor in his Circle. Then word came to me one day that there was a man in your world who had taken an extraordinary amount of interest in my Sis's mediumship. And as time went on I was told this on many occasions. This began eventually to have the effect of making me think whereas all those years ago when my Sis finally came over to my world and I had sworn that I would have nothing further to do with the earth plane , I certainly found myself thinking why throw away all the knowledge I had accumulated over the years and I went along to have a look.

And Raymondo knows that for some time I was in the background so to speak, – yes, in the background by choice, because I was just here to observe – but the day came when I thought 'Well, to hell with it all I shall endeavour to return,' but of course I was uncertain at that stage whether or not I would be able to work through this medium. And that took quite some time and as all the folks here all know – quite a lot of effort and practice, before I was able to manage at first and speak. (*Ray.* That's right.)

Oh yes, – perhaps if you had come two years ago Tom, then you may have simply heard me gasp a word here and gasp a word there (*Tom.* You've done well then.) Yes. I ain't done too bad, (*laughter* – No you ain't!) so that is the answer to your question, Ann. (*Ann.* Thank you, Walter.) I had no intention at first of ever returning to your earth to work in this way but it was through his great interest in my Sis that drew me eventually to him.

Now I'm back with a vengeance – Okay. (*Tom.* Can you say why was the name Margery was chosen, when her name was Mina?) Well, I'll tell you why Tom.. That was a pure invention on the part of 'Birdie'– he chose the name – he wanted to protect her life of course, at first, but the way things worked out everyone in the bloody world knew about her (*much laughter*) That was his suggestion – not mine and not Leroy's either . (*Tom.* Thank you.) He was a very nice gentleman but at the same time he, I suppose, like everyone, had his strange ways. (*Tom.* Yes.) And of course eventually – well not – let's not go into that. (*Tom.* No – We've read the book.) The book – there's been thousands and most of them had no idea what they are speaking of. (*Tom.* No. – like so many books.) Yes, second hand!

Well, I feel as if I could sit here within Stewart and speak to you all night (*Ray.* You're welcome.) We have no limitations of time over here of course. Anything else before I disappear?

Tom. Yes – do you have the choice whether you wish to stay close to the earth plane?

Walter. Had my Sis not embarked on a career as a medium, then the world would never have heard the name Walter Stinson. You know Tom that it is Love which unites people, and draws them together. My Sis and I were always extremely close when I was upon the earth plane – so it was natural that when she began to develop that I would begin again to work with her and of course, this was particularly successful because of the love and sympathy between us. So yes – I did choose very much so to work with her. Who else would I entrust with my Sis's safety but myself? I wish that you had known her. (*Tom.* Would have loved it.) Yes, I'm often with her today. (*Tom.* Is she doing similar kind of work?) No, she wants nothing to do with the whole business – in fact when I am in her company which I often am it is rare that that we discuss the old days of Spiritualism itself. (*Tom.* Do you talk to her about this circle?) Rarely. (*Tom.* Interesting.) It is at the moment still too painful for her. (*Tom.* Understood.) What she gave in 25 or 30 years most mediums give or do not experience in a lifetime.

As I speak to you more and more, week by week I have to say that I find discussing happened in the past not half as bad as I imagined it would be. (*Tom.* Good – it's helping you to work through it?) Yes, it is – it is – and who knows in time perhaps because of this I can help my Sis to overcome it. I think I know it will have been successful when eventually I persuade her to come with me to the circle. (*Tom.* That will be brilliant.) Yes. I think I have held on to the medium long enough. Good night to you all."

This was followed by comments from the sitters "Goodnight Walter – and thank you – Great – Fascinating."

However, this was not quite the end as the "team" wished to use up all the energy and we heard Christopher say "Put your hands on your knees. – Palms up!"

The music was played for a few minutes along with our lah-lah 'singing', then Gaynor said she could feel somebody near her, alongside the cabinet curtain. They were welcomed by the Circle, and Tom's trumpet started moving – Sunrise gave his sign and was welcomed as usual by everyone.

Both trumpets then started moving together all around the room – up to the ceiling and then down to touch some of the sitters – like fireworks. Tom's trumpet rested across his knees like it used to do all those years ago.

Gaynor could feel someone touching her jumper. Then the trumpets deliberately knocked against each other and we could hear the knocking. A large hand was seen over the luminous part of the trumpet – it was confirmed as Walter's – then they circled again extremely fast.

My first experience of seeing what could be done with the trumpet, apart from hearing quiet voices through one was *mesmerising* – the speed at which they could move and the distance they could reach from the medium – far faster than a person could handle them.

The cabinet curtains were drawn together by the spirits – then we heard footsteps – out in the room followed by hands clapping. The trumpets were then knocked on the floor VERY rapidly and noisily for about 10 seconds.

When Michael asked if they would go to his Circle the following night and do the same – and they knocked even louder and faster, he added "I'll keep you to that."

With that demonstration of skill and exuberance the trumpet became still – and after a short interval White Feather closed the circle as usual with "May the Great White Spirit be with you All."

What an evening, so full of love and chat and imparted knowledge – direct as you might say "from the horse's mouth" and not – in Walter's own words – "second hand".

Walter Stinson

and his 'Sis' – Mina

New Vistors to the Circle

In June 1993 Tom had given his talk in Wakefield at the invitation of Joe Cooper, and had stayed overnight with a lovely couple. In the course of the conversation later that evening he discovered that Pat knew about making training videos at the college where she worked. When he ran the idea passed her of making a video of his talk she was enthusiastic and the idea was born.

With Tony, her husband, as the cameraman all they needed was to decide on the venues.

The filming took place throughout the summer of 1994 including the first session in my home, on one hot evening – but all went well – despite the neighbour deciding to mow his lawn in the middle of it while my patio windows were wide open!

As Pat and Tony were staying with us before their trip to film Tom's talk in Middlesbrough the following day, Stewart's circle had agreed that they should witness a 'live' home circle. This was Pat and Tony's first visit to any kind of home circle and neither had had any experience of physical phenomena, although they had read books and had heard, and had now filmed Tom's recent talk – so it was not completely new to them.

Throughout the sitting there was much laughter created by the usual light–hearted banter with our Spirit friends – especially Christopher and Walter. This is always an important ingredient in any successful Home Circle – as this one certainly is. The love, harmony and sincerity are clearly felt by all concerned and frequently remarked upon by our Spirit friends.

Today was the hottest day for five years and we could hear the rumblings of a thunderstorm nearby which could, unfortunately, adversely affect the phenomena... and although the temperature in the room was extremely high, everyone was in good spirits.

When Walter had established himself and been introduced to the visitors , Tony said, "I have had the privilege of reading some of the circle transcripts from Tom and when I read of your presence on these occasions, I had an extremely, strong powerful feeling that you were going to tell us something very important about the world you live in."

Walter. Yes ... you mean this evening sir ? ..

Tony. I don't know whether it is this evening, Walter – and there's no need to refer to me as sir –please call me Tony .. (*laughter.*)

Walter. Then in that case you may refer to me as Walter .. (*more laughter.*) Okay. What I would like to stress , not only to Tony, but also to everyone sitting here, is that what we have managed to accomplish so far within this Circle is merely the beginning. When Tony speaks in terms of something which eventually I shall relate to your world, convey to your world, concerning mine – this is correct – in time there will be much which I shall be able to do, that I want to do – but first we have to establish the reality of my world. Once that has been accepted then we have a programme planned, a programme which we hope will show to people, all the peoples of your world, not only that there is no death, but the very nature of life itself –that's what we want to tell the people of your world – to remove for all time the sting of death. Yes. Does that answer your question Tony? (*Tony.* It answers it very well – thank you) Okay.

Walter. "Pat... how would you like to feel the hand of a man who has been dead for 80 years? (*Pat.* I think it would be marvellous.) I think it would be marvellous for me too ... Raymondo .. will you switch your light on.

Ray switched on the small red light– and June who sits alongside Stewart's right changed places with Pat, and Walter instructed Pat to hold Stewart's hand. And then explained

"In a moment I shall take from Stewart energy which you know and refer to as Ectoplasm, into that I shall dip my etheric hand and this will give to it a temporary physical coating ... for a short time it will be solid to your world and with that hand I shall touch yours ... you understand (*Pat.* Yes.) Okay. All I ask is that you tell all in the Circle what you are experiencing (*Pat.* Yes, I'll do that ...) Wait for a moment, ... Tony – you have no objections ... (*Tony.* No. I think it is a great privilege that this should happen.) *(laughter.)* Good, I promise to touch her nowhere else .. (*more laughter was heard .. especially from Pat.*) Tony, as I always say to people, and I am at pains to point out, although I have been in my world for many years now, I am still very much a man – and you know what I mean .. (*Tony.* Yes .. I understand.) may I congratulate you on your wife sir ... Raymondo, may we have the music please.

After a few minutes Pat then described what was happening. She could feel his hand on her arm and on her hand which was holding Stewart's. (*Pat.* Thank you Walter .. that was wonderful.)

Walter. I'm pleased that I have been able to do this for you .. I suspect that you will get the third degree from Tony .. (*laughter*) Shall we put him out of his misery now ... Tony, would you like to feel my hand also? (*Tony.* I would very much like to.) Okay Raymondo, light please .. Pat, it has been a real pleasure to sit here and hold your hand – I only wish that we could do this all night. (*Pat.* Thank you Walter, it was wonderful.) *(laughter.)* I shall not forget ... Tony, change places with your wife.

Pat and Tony then changed places.

This was unusual as Walter usually only held the hand of the ladies but this is what followed –

Walter. Raymondo, keep the light on ... Tony, take Stewart's hand (Yes ..) Raymondo ... lift your light so that Tony can see the straps on Stewart's hand. ... Tony you are satisfied with those' (*Tony.* Yes, I can see the straps.) Okay. We want to be certain that you have no doubt in your mind (*Tony.* No doubt whatsoever.) Okay. Off with the light Raymondo. ... Peter, you're sitting next to Tony (*Peter.* Yes Walter.) take Tony's hand ... now will the rest of the Circle link their hands together. (*Tom told him he couldn't reach past the camera*) that doesn't matter ... so long as some of you are linked together. Tony, you tell the rest of the Circle what you can feel – don't be nervous (I will do .. I'm not nervous at all.) Okay, on with the music please ... louder..

Tony then described exactly what he felt –the hand moving up and down his arm – pulling his shirt –"a very warm and strong hand – it has considerable strength in it – now tapping me on the arm –

now playing with my wrist watch – I think he's trying to undo it – he's struggling hard to get it off – now he's taken it right off my arm". As Tony said that, Gaynor who sits on the other side of Stewart, said she had got it !!

She felt it put into her hand by Walter! Tony's watch has a leather buckle–type strap, not an expander, which is very difficult to undo. The music stopped and Tony said " Walter, I have never had any doubt there was another world, but I've never had the privilege of being so close to it as this"

Walter. Tony –you've seen nothing yet ! (*Tony*. That's good to know.) Okay. Raymondo, hit the light please .. Tony, you're still happy? (*Tony*. Very happy.)

Tony checked the straps again.

.. Okay off – no just a moment ... Tony change places with June, please ... Gaynor then asked if she should give Tony his watch. Walter replied "No .. it's yours!" (*laughter*)

Gaynor. Is it an apport from Christopher?

Walter. What you chose to do is up to you," he answered. Gaynor then handed the watch back.

Because of the heat and the impending storm, we were told they were having problems with the ectoplasm but they were able to continue with the experiments and that evening we heard voices through the trumpets – both Tom's and the circle's own.

Sunrise spoke briefly – rather slowly but quite loudly "Woooff ... just a minute ... just a minute, (*Tom*. Yes ... that's Sunrise like he used to be all those years ago.) so good to be here tonight .. Wooof.. Tom... son ... Tom ... son ... (*Tom*. Yes Sunrise.) me here... (*Tom*. Yes, I know. Thank you ..) Woooff.. "

The trumpet then went down to the floor and everyone commented how good he had been ... "Well done ... Wonderful that, Sunrise ... Excellent ... The best I've heard through the trumpet ... so clear .."

Christopher asked "Tony ... (*Tony*. Yes Christopher.) are you shattered yet ? Are you mystified and puzzling and things like that ? (*laughter*.) Are you shocked ? (*Tony*. No, I'm not shocked, I'm enthralled actually ..) Uncle Tony ... what's it mean exactly? ...(*Tony.* Really fascinating .. very, very interesting.)

With the trumpets continuing to move around in the air, very close to me I heard a voice – "Norman." (*Ann.* Yes, my love ...) "how are you ... (*Ann.* I'm fine ..) I'm trying ... can you hear me .. (*Ann.* I can hear you very well ..). You haven't been well .. (*Ann.* No, but I'm a lot better now.) .. Look after yourself, love .." We then heard four or five loud kissing noises (*Ann.* Lovely .. thank you .. well done.)

The other sitters confirmed that the voice was coming through both trumpets and Christopher immediately popped in to say that they were trying to put it through both!

Another step forward despite the atmospheric conditions.

It really was all stops out (to coin a phrase) for the benefit of Pat and Tony who were doing so much to make Tom's video possible. And that evening there was another step forward when after showing the ectoplasm forming by Stewart's chin the light was put on again to see Stewart's face apparently changing as a face appeared and we heard a voice say.

"I want to speak with Pat. (*Pat.* Yes.) ... can you hear me ... (*Pat.* Yes, I can ... you're doing ever so well ...) it's me ... (*Pat.* Yes?) my girl .. (*Pat.* You're doing very well .. come on ..) *(the voice then came much stronger*) .. " I wish I could do so much better than this .. I want to speak to my girl .. (*Pat.*: DAD ! ... Dad ...) Yes .. Pat ... (*Pat.* Oh, Dad .. it's wonderful to hear you.) Where's my girl ... (*Pat.* I'm here Dad .. I'm here.) I've waited ... now ... for this moment ... (*Pat.* Oh, Dad. thank you for coming.) My girl ... ! don't know if you can hear me .. (*Pat.* Yes, I can .. perfectly.) I want my girl.. (*Gaynor.* Do you want her hands?) Yes.

Both of Stewart's arms were raised towards Pat and she moved over to hold them ... (*Pat.* It's wonderful of you to come ... you said you would didn't you ... thank you. I'm so happy.)

Pat was almost overcome as she again thanked her Dad for coming to see her ..

Dad. I'm all right now ... I'm well now ... (*Pat.* Are you playing golf?) Of course ... I loved you so much .. (*Pat.* I know you did, Dad.) you've done so well .. (*Pat.* Thank you ..) I'm always with you

.. (He then blew a kiss .. (*Pat.*I know you are Dad ..) as the voice faded Pat then moved back to her seat.

Walter immediately returned through Stewart: "I think we ought to bring our meeting to a close – before I do so may I just say to Pat – your father tried so very hard and he is so happy and delighted. (*Pat.* Thank you Walter.) Okay Listen folks ... I think you will probably agree that it would not be wise for us to continue any further .. (*All.* Right.) Okay. ... We have taken more energy and power from you than we had expected to do ... in view of the conditions ... I shall stay no longer. I look forward greatly to the future."

Such a special night not only for Pat and Tony – now both in that World of Spirit, but also for me to hear how trumpets are really meant to be used and to see a good transfiguration of a face which was recognised and could speak to his daughter, with such love.

Much of the script here has been taken from Tom's transcript of the time, with additions by me, refreshing my memory listening to the cassette from that evening. *(now safely digitally stored.)*

Summer celebrations 1994 with our friends Pat and Tony Hamblin

More Experiences in a New Circle

Through a number of coincidences early in 1994 we were also invited to sit in a family Home Circle in West Yorkshire. They were just getting started and already had had phenomena around the house.

The five of us sat in a curtained off section of their L-shaped lounge-diner round a large dining table. From the first time we sat together the table responded to questions by juddering "Yes" to a positive suggestion. 5-feet long (150cm) and weighing 85 pounds (38.5 kilos), it soon began to twitch and as the weeks went by it began to rock, wiggle, lift and dance.

We had put various things on the table for the 'children' to play with—little temple bells, a tambourine, wooden spoon and a rattle and they discovered they could move them by shimmying the table to inch them across the surface, but when the table was really dancing those wouldn't move. They would stay in a straight line in the middle of the table, A chalk line had been ruled across the table, so we'd know if they had moved. They never shifted across unless the spirit children wanted them to move and then they would shuffle across and fall off on to somebody's knee – but in the early days my little long handled bell never moved.

Sometimes the others were picked up and rung, but not mine. Why? – probably because I'd put some luminous tape on the long handle and they couldn't hold it. Later they loved to pick it up and swing it around.

When they started to spell out answers to our questions by rocking the table the number of times required for the letter I became known as the 'Alphabet lady'. It was decided that I should ask "Before M?" – "After M?" and wait for the response and then I would call out the letters, waiting briefly between each until the table responded to the letter wanted in the Alphabet. A-B-C … laborious but it did save the energy, so they could do more in a sitting. We had many messages that way but later they decided they could use the spoon like a drumstick and tap the table, so instead of spelling out the messages by moving the table, which took a lot of energy, because they could lift the spoon up and move it about why not use the spoon to tap them out. The spoon was marked with a tiny spot of luminous paint on the tip of the underside of the bowl.

One night, the spoon appeared right in front of my face going 1,2,3,4 - pause -1- pause - 1,2,3,4 – DAD. The spoon moved rapidly up and down saying "Yes!" and I came out with the wonderful words, "The spoon's nodding its head!" – A never to be forgotten statement!

That was the fun that we had in those early days and built a rapport with the team of children who came to "play". We discovered all their names and their ages and sang Nursery Rhymes and children's songs, like 'The Wheels on the Bus go round and round' and 'Chitty Chitty Bang Bang' etc. to which they made the table move.

As we sang many of the old Music Hall songs like 'Roll out the Barrell', 'Knees up Mother Brown' etc we found we had a troupe of Music Hall entertainers joining in with the dancing of the table — and eventually it even danced the 'Can-can'—and woe betide you if you started lah-lah-ing the tune too soon. Tom often did and the table would stop and would not move. When he'd apologised, it would rock to tap 1-2-3 and then we were allowed to join in with 'dah da-da-da dah' and to sit there with this 5-foot long dining table rocking and lifting, back and forth (under our hands), I know it's a bit mind blowing but it did happen, week after week. I sat at one end of the table so I know how much my hands lifted alternately. Over the weeks of movement the legs became loose and P--- , the man of the house, had to tighten the nuts holding them on a number of times.

Eventually as development progressed, we were told to take the large table out of the circle, as they wanted space to be able to move around and it was replaced with a small stool for the pad and bells. I felt the 'fur' of a large dog pass across my legs and when I commented on it, I heard the guide say, in a very deep voice, beside me – "My robes." It was Grey Wolf on the move!

This main guide later asked us to remove the spare chair that was placed between the medium and me so that he had space to stand. This was an indication that they had some solidity, as we found when they would use the 'trumpet' to tap the form on the head and then all the way down the body. We could see the movement by the luminous tabs on the metal trumpet and hear the sound as contact was made.

On the day we arranged to take reconstruction photos of how we first sat it seems that the folks in spirit had a few surprises for us.

Here is the first part of A---a's official report from that day:

Home Circle Saturday July 8th 1995

I must first relate 'events' which happened before the sitting began.

Tom and Ann had come over from Hull slightly earlier, to take some photos of how the circle arrangements were when we first began sitting with the large dining table.

As we all took our original places around the table, the table began to vibrate ... first steadily, then continuously!

We all lifted our hands off the table and the vibrating and nudging still continued.

We all began talking, saying how wonderful this was, when the table lifted up at J---'s side, causing the bells to slide over to A---a!

We replaced them and sang a few songs, hoping that we might be able to photograph the table up to its old tricks again, but it only managed to lift up the once!

A photograph was taken of where the bells ended up on the table.

Amazingly enough all this took place before we had darkened the room .. it was in broad daylight!

We sat talking round the table for awhile, and it continued to vibrate and move to confirm what we were speaking about!

Whilst we were hanging the curtains and generally getting ready for the circle, there were a number of knocks and taps on the other side of the room door!

As we sat to reconstruct how we started sitting, the table started to shimmy in full daylight.

When it finally stopped moving this was the result .

As we were hanging the curtains that evening, we had Telekinesis in FULL daylight when the roll of sticky black tape was thrown across room. Every week we had to seal the large patio windows in the living area with blackout curtaining sealing the sides with insulating tape. As I was doing this, Tom was fixing a curtain at the other end of the room and asked for the tape. As I put my hand up on to the table to throw it to Tom, it took off and landed beside him.

The rest of the evening was just as energetic with the cabinet curtain being vigorously wafted about. Many lights were seen in different colours and a number of visitors were felt moving about and two were 'felt' to sit in the chair between J--- and Tom. We heard the pencil writing on the pad and at the end of the circle found a number of initials of our visitors.

On one rare occasion, in total darkness, J--- , the medium was levitated to ceiling with her chair. She came out of trance while her head was touching the ceiling, before descending slowly. We knew of her position by her voice. An un-nerving experience for her.

Many times we had little lights shining and moving around the room – spirit lights – coming and going.

Voices were heard. Usually in the early days they would speak through the medium, but in their own tones and accent. Occasionally, if the voice was extremely quiet, they would use a 'trumpet' megaphone. Later some voices were independent of the medium and came from anywhere in the room – a very special advance in the circle's progress. Moving across the space above us whenever they liked.

The Summer of '95 was particularly busy for the members of the team in charge of telekinesis. Trumpets were flattened when a Grandfather who was a blacksmith wanted to show us he was present.

One very warm evening in late July a towel was thrown into cabinet from the empty chair when a spirit visitor wanted to sit down (the towel was there in case anyone needed to wipe their face). Later when we felt more forms moving around in the room A---a said, "Take a seat why

We heard the trumpets being battered into these shapes.

don't you." (there was a spare chair for 'visitors' between Tom and
J---.) They literally did – they placed it in the centre of the circle
facing A---a who had invited them!

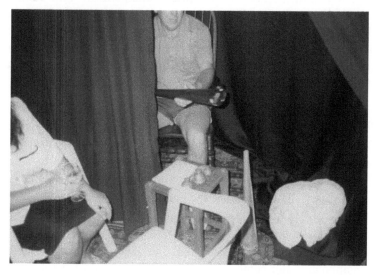

*... and in the process of moving the stool as well, slightly flattened
the trumpet again, which finished up in the cabinet with P---.*

On anther occasion the Bureau drawers (alongside the cabinet)
were pulled open and a heavy brass greyhound ornament was moved
from on top of the display cabinet across room to the floor by the
bureau – soundlessly!

We had several changes of taped music for the circle over the
years but this one seemed to be spirit selected.

J--- had felt compelled to buy a tape of Irish music while out
shopping one week and this is how A---a recorded it in her report:

"A tape recording of lilting Irish music had been made during
the week, and J--- removed the 'Fairy Ring', tape from the right-
hand cassette of the large cassette recorder (which is on the floor
at her right) and replaced it with the Irish music in case our spirit
friends wished it to be played.

The usual circle music tape was in the left-hand cassette [deck] of the cassette recorder, and sometimes, Ann is able to make out a tiny red glow from the little light on the left cassette [deck] whilst this tape is playing. Any tape that is put in the left-hand cassette deck will be played over and over until it is manually stopped ... hence the tiny red light – to show that that side has 'continuous play' facilities, whereas the right-hand cassette deck does not. There is a good amount of black tape which completely covers the red light and the lid of left-hand cassette deck, so that it is impossible to remove a tape from that side without peeling the tape off to enable the 'lid' of the cassette deck to be opened up.

The circle began just before 8pm and Tom opened in prayer. We managed to sing three lines of 'Pop Goes the Weasel' before our spirit friends started the Irish music tape off playing!

The trumpet rose up in the air and danced around in front of everyone. A tune came on which J--- didn't know, and because she wasn't singing, the trumpet went over to her and gave her a knock on her head!

The wooden spoon rose up and 'danced' around in the air with the trumpet.

The spoon then went down to the table and the trumpet, which was still in the air, knocked it gently to show us that it had been put down on the table.

When J--- joked that our spirit friends had impressed her to buy the Irish tape because she didn't know the songs and therefore couldn't sing along, the trumpet went to her and knocked her head again!

The trumpet swung around the room in a large circular movement, and when A---a said it looked like a huge Catherine Wheel, the trumpet moved in front of her and the bell-end spun round at a furious rate to simulate a small Catherine Wheel. ...

When 'The Spinning Wheel' was played, the trumpet whizzed around the room in tiny circles until the tune finished, whereupon it went down to the floor and settled there. There were stamping noises which both Ann and A---a said could have been from inside the cabinet ... they were certainly from that direction. ...

There were more stamping noises in the space between J--- and Ann, and there was a very loud stamp in front of J---. The stamping gradually became faster, until it sounded just like horses galloping.

At this point, Ann said that she could see a dull red glow from the cassette machine, but she didn't think that there was a red light at the right-hand deck (which was the one that the Irish music tape had been put in at the start of the circle.)

There were some rapid taps on the table-top and more loud, quick stamps."

Were they acknowledging what I had seen and the red light was on?

At this point J--- went into trance and what followed was a wonderful evidence for me.

Here is how A---a recorded it:

"Whilst 'I'll take you home again, Kathleen' was playing, a gentleman's voice was heard attempting to sing along with us. It gradually became louder but it wasn't very clear. It was a very deep sounding voice, and when it stopped, Grey Wolf greeted us.

Tom. Lovely! There's a great crowd tonight ...

Ann. Were you singing with us, tonight?

GW. No ... he not use Janet ... just her power ...

All. That's good.

Tom. So, are you speaking through Janet or independent?

GW. ME use Janet ...

A---a. Right, and the other person used Mum's power to enable him to speak?

GW. Yes ... he knew Ann many years ago ... you must think ... he cannot speak yet but he sang ...

Ann. Lovely, I'll think about that ...

GW. He sang to people ... you knew of him ... your Auntie ...

Ann. Auntie Evie?

GW. Yes, little lady ... she liked him ... he sang to her then, he sing to her now.

Ann. That's lovely.

GW. Lullabies ... he says to say lullabies

Ann. Yes, that's right, Lovely.

A---a. Can I ask a question Grey Wolf, please?

GW. What if I say no?

A---a. If you say no? I shall fall out with you!!

GW. Oh no ... you ask!

A---a. Well, it's what everybody was talking about earlier, I just wanted to ask ....

GW. ... . Yes, they can come.

A---a. Right, I just wanted to okay it with you and make sure.

GW . Yes

Tom. I was just going to ak the same thing!

GW. Tom, great minds think alike ..... Stop there!!

Tom. Yes, okay!"

It had been arranged for Sydney and Gladys to visit the circle, and we needed permission from Grey Wolf first and here it was.

The man who had sung was my maternal Grandfather. He died when I was just 10 months old, so I didn't remember him but I had heard of him from my Auntie Evie, his daughter, to whom he used to sing 'I'll take you home again, Kathleen'. She loved him so very much. Such a special contact for me. (55 years after his passing.)

The circle continued for a good thirty minutes more including a session with P--- for us to see the progress in the development of the transfiguration phenomena. It was an amazing session. We recorded seeing moustaches, dark skin, and face with beard resembling Sir William Crookes and J--- at one point recognised her father. There were many different changes of features and they were very clear.

After we had closed the circle we eagerly examined the cassette player. This what A---a wrote:

"When the lights were switched on after the circle, we saw that the Irish music tape was in the cassette which has the 'continuous play' facility ... where the original circle music tape had been! This accounts for Ann being able to see the glow of the little red light. So, somehow, without us knowing it, or even hearing, the original circle music tape and the Irish music tape had been switched over in the cassette-machine, which must have happened in the time between the lights being switched off and the Irish music tape being set off playing.

The interesting thing is that, as mentioned before, the cassette which has the continuous play facility is usually used for the original circle music tape (which is left in the player all the time) and there is a lot of tape over the red Light and the door of this cassette, which means that all this tape must be pulled off before you can [physically] open the door of the cassette, however, none of the tape had been pulled off or disturbed in any way whatsoever!"

What 'phenomenal' spirit transposition!

The proposed visit of Sydney and Gladys Shipman took place as arranged the following week.

We had had a number of instances of Spirit writing appearing on the note pad. This evening the pad was placed on the small card table together with the bells, and a small glass dome in the centre of it.

On this occasion, in September 1996, when Tom's old friends, Sydney and Gladys Shipman, from their circle days in Middlesbrough, came to sit they received both an apport and a special note to go with it.

Tom charging the luminous spots on the trumpets before use

That was a special evening and spirit pulled out all the stops, in thanks for all Sydney and Gladys had done over many years. The previous week the spirit team had asked that Tom bring his trumpet to the circle for this special evening, and it was put to good use.

When we sang 'Catch the Sunshine', both trumpets rose up into the air and slowly moved around in front of everyone. At the same time as the bell-end of one trumpet was facing Gladys, the bell-end of the other trumpet faced Syd.

One trumpet knocked J---'s head to show us that she was still in her seat and then both trumpets swayed and bobbed about the room, criss-crossing each other and 'snaking' around each other, banging against each other every now and then.

Both trumpets 'danced' about and kept time with our singing, and they knocked against each other in an "ay tiddly ay ty, ty ty" sequence – the signature tune of Sam (Glady's father), who was a frequent communicator in Tom's Mum's circle of which both Syd and Gladys had been members.

One of the trumpets moved to the table and very gently tapped the glass dome.

When we sang 'When the Roll is called up Yonder', the trumpets knocked against each other twice at the end of each line of the chorus and at the end of the song, one trumpet banged twice on the ceiling. – As singers would have clapped when singing it.

The trumpets moved over to A---a and when she suggested singing 'The World Hath felt ... ', they both moved up and down for 'yes'. When we sang this, both trumpets kept time for us.

One trumpet then moved over to the space between J--- and Ann and tapped the head of a spirit person who was standing there. The trumpet then moved down both sides of the person, tapping against 'him' all the time to show us how solidly they had been able to build.

Then, there were tapping noises on the trumpet, which was in front of her, level with her face. When asked, it was confirmed via the trumpets that they were actually being held by spirit people in the room, it wasn't just the psychic power which was being used to move them about.

The trumpet moved around the room clockwise and anti-clockwise and we heard a 'whoof' sound from it ... this was Sunrise, who always makes the 'two-way' circle sign when he is present.

The trumpet tapped the medium's head again to let us know she was in her place. It then moved in front of Gladys and the first spirit person to speak through it was her father, Sam.

Syd.I was hoping you'd come here.

Sam. Yes ...

Gladys. Is my mother with you?

46

Sam. Yes ... ALL are here.

S & G. Good, that's good.

The trumpet then rested on one edge of the table, and at this point. there were more breathing noises from the trumpet, and after the communicator tried a few times, we managed to catch her name ... Esther. The trumpet moved to the table and rested on it for a while before our communicator spoke again ....

Tom. Mam's sister, Esther? (The trumpet moved up and down for 'yes'.) That's Lovely; Esther and Lily sang a duet through the trumpet in our circle.

Ann. asked, "Is Lily here as well?" (The trumpet moved side to side for 'no'.)

Tom. Haven't had Esther before ... have you come with Mam and Aunt Agg?

The trumpet again moved up and down for 'yes'.

A----a saw a tiny, sparkling light about halfway along the trumpet. Everyone then saw something dark moving over the luminous tabs on the trumpet. It looked like a finger, and when the trumpet was in front of me, I actually saw a hand which was lit up by the glow of luminosity from the luminous tabs on the trumpet.

The trumpet tapped against the corner of the table by J---. and then moved down to the floor in front of A---a where it rolled a little before staying upright and still.

We then heard Grey Wolf's voice ....

GreyWolf. Peace and Love ...

All. Peace and Love, Grey Wolf ... it's been a wonderful evening!

GW. It is wonderful to see our lady and gentleman ...

Gladys. Oh, thank you very much.

Syd. We're pleased to come ... it was nice of you to ask us, and we wish you every success.

GW. We are so happy you were able to come here ... we want to thank you so much from our side for helping those many years ago.

Syd. Well, it's work we felt obliged to do.

GW. I won't speak long ... we want to try all things tonight ...

And they did!

When we 'dah-dah'd' the 'Cancan', both trumpets rose up into the air again and knocked against each other repeatedly. One trumpet knocked against the door at the very end of the song. There were some quiet stamps in the space between J--- and Ann, and when we sang 'Knees Up Mother Brown' Grey Wolf could be heard chanting along for part of the song. ....

The tape which was recording the circle came to the end of side one, and when A---a asked if our spirit friends were able to turn it over Grey Wolf answered 'Yes'.

Before, if they have been conserving the power for other things, the small tape recorder has been pushed into A---a's hands for her to turn the tape over and set it off recording again. We all heard the tape being turned over and the button pressed to set off again.

The Irish taped music was then turned down, and we heard little Jenny as she sang 'Twinkle, Twinkle Little Star' for us through the 'talkbox' (as Grey Wolf calls it!)

All. Well done! Lovely!

Jenny. Want to blow a kiss to the Lady ...

A---a. Off you go, then!

We heard Jenny blowing a kiss to Gladys and Gladys blew one back to her.

The Irish taped music was turned up again and we heard Sam knocking out his 'ay tiddly ay tye, tye-tye' signature tune on the small table-top.

The little cowbell was lifted and rung, and then it fell to the floor, hitting my knee on the way down. There were more solid, heavy knocks on the table, and when Gladys said that she couldn't hear the tapping noises on the glass dome, our spirit friends turned the music down and tapped again on the glass dome so that she could hear it!

Immediately after this, both Syd and Gladys were touched by what felt like a solid finger.

There were clicking sounds in front of me, but we couldn't tell how they were being made. ...and Syd was touched again on his arm and his knee was tapped a number of times.

Before the circle, someone had said, 'Wouldn't it be lovely if Syd and Gladys were touched tonight!'

I saw a tiny golden light where the medium was sitting, and suddenly, the writing pad was flung towards Syd and Gladys, and it landed across Syd's left arm and Gladys's right arm. Gladys kept hold of it for the rest of the sitting.

Then I saw another light near the medium and Tom saw a dark shape which shot across the room from the door towards Syd and Gladys.

Suddenly a voice came out of the darkness: 'Gladys ... Mrs Ellerby ... '

Gladys. Hello there.

Tom. Do you know a Mrs Ellerby?

Gladys. Only in the body.

Voice. 'Not well .... send thoughts ....'

Gladys. Yes, alright.

Tom. Who's telling us this?

Voice. 'Margaret.'

Gladys. Right, I'll do what you say, and I'll enquire ... I know the lady well enough.

Margaret's voice sounded to have been in front of Tom and Gladys, well away from the medium.

A—a. Yes, hello ...

GW. Tried to do much tonight. ..

Gladys. You've worked very hard, haven't you?

GW. More people ... more physical. Thank you so much for coming and for giving your power to help this circle.

Gladys. Thank you for having us.

GW. My love goes with you both ... I leave gifts ... Peace and Love.

All. Peace and love, Grey Wolf.

Another communicator went on to pass more thanks to Gladys from those who had already passed over.

I closed in prayer and when the light was put on, we saw that the wooden spoon was on the floor underneath the table. All the bells on the table were out of position, and the little cowbell was on the floor by the table.

The presents for Syd and Gladys were:

A 1957 sixpence which had been placed underneath the glass dome on the table, – and a written message on the writing pad, referring to the sixpenny piece:

"A good day's pay for a good day's work."

Sydney and Gladys with their 'gifts' The sixpence is still under the dome.

What an evening for our visitors, voices through the trumpet, independent voices through a 'talk-box', being touched by what felt like finger and then to receive a message through spirit writing and an apport – phenomena just as they had in the circle 40-50 years before.

* * * * *

Unfortunately, a few months later, because of health problems and pressure of work, this Home Circle closed, which was quite a loss to us all.

A Sitting Away from Home

The visit of Sydney and Gladys to the Home Circle followed this successful sitting in their home in Robin Hoods Bay on the North Yorkshire coast the previous year in the hot summer of '95.

The medium and her husband had gone with us to give these long-time workers for spirit a trip back to the days of the Minnie Harrison Home Circle which had been held in their own home in Middlesbrough. Sydney was by then 91 years old and Gladys was 79. They had kept contact with the other members of the Saturday Night Club who had passed into spirit by sitting every week with a home made Ouija board, which has now been gifted to me.

Whenever Tom and I visited them we always had a sitting with them with Tom and me in charge of the planchette.

This is Tom's report of that day:

"We sat in Syd and Gladys' lounge and although we tried to black out the window, but because of the brightness outside there was still some light penetrating the curtains. This made it very difficult for our spirit friends, but as usual they did their best.

J--- and Tom sat with their backs to the piano with an empty chair between them. Syd and Gladys sat on the settee opposite and P--- sat to the left of J---, and Ann sat at the other end of the "circle'.

After singing the usual three opening songs, J--- was in trance. Tom felt the chair between them move and knock against his leg. A spirit person was heard and felt to sit in it. As we sang Grey Wolf's song 'She'll be coming round the mountain' we heard Grey Wolf humming / chanting his rhythm in time. He gave his opening greeting "Peace and Love" and explained that the light conditions made it difficult but they would do their best in the different surroundings.

He told us the whole of the Saturday Night Club was there and asked that we sing again. We started singing 'We do like to be beside the Seaside' and he cut in to tell us that we were beside the sea – very good, much laughter. Tom then felt the chair moving again and sensed someone was sitting there. It proved to be Sam Hildred, Gladys' Dad who had been very excited during our sitting the previous evening in West Yorkshire by banging the trumpets together- Aye tiddley aye, tye, bong, bong. (his signature tune).

After we sang 'Lambeth Way' we heard light notes being played on the piano at the top end, which Sydney could not hear at. first .... but they got louder and then Sam played his signal quite loudly down at the base end. He repeated it and everyone was very happy.

'Well done Sam.' said Syd, who heard it clearly. Sam played it several times and then spoke quietly through J---. "Wonderful" he said, "things not too good." Gladys gave him encouragement "not easy .... trying so hard.. I'm here ... Are you well?"

"Yes" said Gladys "you are, aren't you?"

"Yes top form.... we're all here..." He found it difficult through a different medium but he had done very well. When Tom said that maybe he was sitting here, there was a heavy thump on the floor, indicating that was indeed where Sam was.

Grey Wolf then told us he had needed to stay close to the power – between J--- and P--- .

We heard a light tap on the 'guest's' chair. These proved to be made by Mona (Gladys's younger sister) and they got faster and louder. After more encouragement she managed to speak quietly "I'm at home – this is home now." Tom asked whether she was still looking after Prudence. "Not now. I'm teaching about communication by thoughts."

We joked about age and Mona said "Bodies may be old, but minds are young.... Douglas is trying to do his lights."

Gladys thought she saw a tiny light over by the end of the piano which Mona confirmed with an excited "Yes ... yes .. tell him if you see lights."

When Gladys said it was difficult especially for his first time Mona said "No.. He is here many times." and Gladys explained she meant it was the first time in a circle of this kind in the house, although she often sees them before she goes to bed – which Mona confirmed.

Gladys thanked them for being around and Mona said the lights would get bigger. She then said Douglas was trying to show Syd a light because he has difficulty in hearing them speaking so to watch for a light near the piano. We then heard finger clicks similar to those we hear on a Saturday night. Gladys heard them quite clearly also. We then heard more notes being played on the piano.

Another communicator from our Saturday night sittings, Beryl, came speaking in her quiet and gentle voice. She was a biologist at Edinburgh University in the 1920s. We introduced her to Syd and Gladys and she said she was pleased to meet them "It is a lovely atmosphere here ... it is a little difficult, but we are doing quite well." We all agreed.

"It is so kind of you to allow us to bring our friends to your home." ... Gladys replied "It is very kind of them to come– with such a long journey."

Beryl then said a lady called Ethel was there. Gladys wondered whether it was Ethel Ingham or perhaps a relative but it was neither and Beryl told us she was getting a little upset. Tom felt it was probably his cousin Ethel Farthing (Bessant) known to us as 'Our Eth' who was so close to Tom's Mam, Minnie. Beryl immediately confirmed this and said the lady had brought her. Gladys then remembered her quite well as she used to go and help Gladys and Edith Nellist clean Grange Road Spiritualist Church each week for many years - especially in memory of 'Aunt Min'. Ethel was 91 when she passed in January 1992. Beryl said she may have been old in body but not in mind.

"Very true" remarked Tom. "She was always very lively to talk to although in her latter years she was unable to walk unaided being crippled with arthritis." Beryl said this was how Eth said Gladys is now – not old in thought.

Within a few minutes Douglas controlled J---, and said he had tried to bring the lights this afternoon but couldn't quite make it.

"I've tried many times .. to show you .. strange for me to talk ... many years since .."

Gladys: You've still got plenty of work have you, Douglas?

Douglas. Plenty, they call me the professor... I try things with power. _

Gladys. Yes we have seen one or two unusual lights ...

Douglas. Have to go .

Shortly after we heard someone playing on the strings inside the piano which Syd was able to hear. There was more tapping which sounded like playing with the pedals .. then Sam gave his sign again and played some chords as well.

As Syd said he'll soon be able to accompany the singing. There was more finger clicking.

Grey Wolf then spoke "Sorry we have to go now... we wanted to do much more.... God bless you all... Peace and love."

That was a very special visit for us all and for the team to work so well under difficult lighted conditions, and a tribute to the power and devotion of the medium and her husband.

My Hand Kissed and Medium Unbound

By 1995 Stewart's circle had moved venue, to a larger space for the séance room and the spirit team had decided to try a new format for sitting in order to protect the medium when there were visitors to the circle who had not sat before. The regular sitters were to sit in a line across the room blocking access to the medium and it was at one of these sittings I had my next experience of the phenomena.

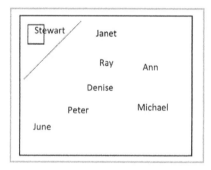

This was the first time I had been allowed to sit without Tom being present so I felt it was quite an honour.

Diagram of the seating plan for June 27th 1995.

For the first part of the sitting, quiet, peaceful, music was played softly, some knockings heard on the window board, wall and radiator (rather loudly). The seat cushion was picked up and held level with Stewart's chest with the light being switched on and off and moved about. This was a new device with the warning light showing us whether the medium had moved out of his chair. The medium hadn't moved but the spirit team had moved the cushion from under him! The music was also turned off and on by spirit. The seat cushion's use was not continued.

Stewart's luminous knee tabs were removed and stuck to the wall either side of the cabinet just beyond the curtains and at one stage the curtains were drawn across in front of Stewart.

Energy was being taken from Peter, June and Denise, so they were 'out of it'. Ray, Janet, Michael and I were 'awake'– just – but I was yawning excessively, which is spirit's way of taking my energy when it is needed.

After the tape music had been rewound Walter came through and asked for it to be played louder and for us to 'sing' along to whip up the vibrations.

Janet was now also well 'off'. Ray was asked to move the trumpets out of the circle and place them behind me.

June, who was now fully alert, felt a hand, then 2 hands, on her head and then on the back of her neck – she could feel what she thought was the 'curtain' down the side of her – but the curtain hadn't moved out as we could see that the tab on the wall was not obscured – and then she heard Walter talking to her very close by! As Walter moved away from her I saw a greenish haze by her side, only about a foot high and four feet from the ground.

Peter felt a touch on his leg and we heard shuffling feet.

The drumsticks were picked up and a tattoo beaten – Ray was tapped on the head with them and we heard Walter's voice, high up, away from Stewart.

Heavy footsteps were heard and the music tape player was picked up and the volume turned right up.

Right in front of me and to the side of Ray I heard Walter's voice. He asked me to stand and stretch out my arms. As I did, my hands were held by very large hands, my two hands were put together and held by a left hand. The back of my left hand was tapped firmly and audibly, with another hand. He then bent forward and kissed the back of my hands just below the base of the thumbs. The touch was warm, strong and soft and clearly heard as well as felt.

"You may sit down now" – but I already was back in my chair, overwhelmed and wonderstruck – elated. When I say "bent forward" I could sense/hear the movement of him.

There was more movement, then we heard "cannot continue to hold on."

Within a very short time White Feather closed the circle.

The variations in phenomena did not stop there as six months later, after the circle had had a refreshing two-month break, I had a lot on my mind and in the circle that evening I received a rebuke from Christopher:

"How's Ann ? (*Ann.* Very well thank you Christopher ..) yeh .. you're looking very well ... you've been a bit worried or something ... (*Ann.* I've been very, very busy and rather worried.) have you .. *(Ann.* yes ..) thought so 'cos you've brought a bit of it into the room with you ... (*Ann.* Sorry .. I'll try and get rid of it ..) Yeh ... I know it's not your fault ... I know it's easy for me to say 'cos we just come along and nowt worries us but because you live in your world you have different pressures and worries ... we understand that (*Ann.* Good.) but do try and leave them all outside when you come in here .. (*Ann.* Yes ..) (*Ray.* I must be ready to come over there Christopher ..) bloody 'ell ... not yet ... (*laughter*)

Christopher. Ann .. that's better now ... (*Ann.* Good ... sorry Christopher.) No. it isn't your fault cock ... it was kind of a bit thick with you ... but it's all right now ..(*Ann.* Thank you ..)

How are you Uncle Tom? ... (*Tom.* Fine thank you, Christopher ... I keep locking Ann in to get on with her studies ...) Yeh ... it's important ... just want you to know something Uncle Tom ... I don't really need to remind you of this ... but just for you to know that we're always there with you... (*Tom.* Thank you very much.) In fact a few of you have brought a few worries in with you tonight ... Auntie Gaynor isn't much better ... (*laughter.*) I've just said to Uncle Tom, Auntie Gaynor., you tend to forget .. but it applies to you all ... I know you might not always be aware and you might tend to forget sometimes but just remember that we're always there .. (*Gaynor.* Thank you Christopher...) I'm going to do something to make you laugh and buck you up a bit .. she needs a bit of bucking up does Auntie Gaynor ....

We forget that all our energies are needed when we sit and to be preoccupied with our earthly thoughts obviously does interfere with what the spirit world are able to do.

As Louis Armstrong sang:

"Grab your coat grab your hat, Leave your worries on the doorstep. Just direct your feet, on the sunny side of the street."

So you have a picture of how we were sitting that evening, Gaynor was back with us and sitting next to Stewart, while Janet had moved to Denise's place (*in the diagram on p 54*) and as Michael wasn't present she and Tom were sitting alongside me on the "back row".

After chatting for some time with Walter on various circle matters and then with Christopher again, he wished us 'Goodnight' but within a minute we heard someone else, with great difficulty, trying to speak through Stewart – " Can .. you .. hear .. my .. voice .. (*All. Yes*) ... Dick .. Tom .. it's Dick .."

At this point I felt something hit me and land in my lap. It proved to be one of the ropes which had been fastening Stewart to his chair.

As 'Dick' continued to chat to Tom *another* rope landed across my knees. and as Dick finished speaking, a long rope was thrown around Tom's and my shoulders – linking us together*.

'Dick' was followed almost immediately by a lady, speaking very quietly. It was Tom's mother and she was followed by Mr. Jones both passing on brief messages to him.

When Stewart came out of trance, his first comment was that he was to his amazement no longer roped in.

Tom then closed in prayer and we found the ropes were all around Tom and myself and one on Denise too. As we were still sitting in the new format, with Denise, Tom and I on the row behind the main regular sitters, the ropes must have been pitched high, over the heads of those on the front row.

*Rather apt really as Tom had finally moved in with me and we were now 'together' permanently – and it seemed that Spirit approved.

The Importance of Keeping the Contact

Just two weeks later, two of the sitters had gone on holiday, two more had to work and so couldn't make it. In their commitment to the circle this is understood. So that night only Denise and Tom and I were there to sit with Stewart. Sitting in a straight line we were welcomed by Walter.

"Okay friends, can you hear me? (*Tom.* loud and clear.) I shall only be with you for a short while tonight ... there are certain experiments which we would like to try (*Tom.* Just with four of us? ... Okay, that's good.) What we lose in numbers we more than make up for in harmony – (*Tom.* Thank you.) ... of course it would be nice to see a full circle but we do understand ... We wish to at least thank you few folks for coming to allow us this evening to push forward with the development ... and a special thank you to Denise, of course... (*Denise.* Okay, you're more than welcome.). ... Okay ... we may ask you to do something in a short while but please await our instructions ... (*Denise.* Of course.) ... we hope you will have something to take away with you to make the others envious .. (*laughter* ... Great / thank you.) ... Okay, we'll have to see what can be done ... no promises of course. .. (*Tom.* Yes ..) My ... for the past two meetings I have had some difficulty in communicating ... but strangely this evening I find it so much simpler (*Ann.* Good.) Okay, it's often the case when one hopes to be able to communicate well, one finds great difficulty ... encounters great difficulty ... and this evening when I do not intend to say much it is the opposite ... (*laughter*) yes ... lovely harmony folks ... lovely harmony ..."

Walter was immediately followed by a lady, speaking for the first time. She told us she wouldn't reveal who she was until she was sure that her voice sounded as she wanted it to sound. She was a very precisely spoken lady who told us she was not comfortable speaking through the male organ – (but that is not the word she used one night!).

She came several times like that until she felt really comfortable and finally revealed her name as Freda Johnson. She had been a teacher and she had watched the circle from the spirit world – watched these people gathering for years until she felt comfortable; then on one occasion she suddenly spoke to them and said something, suggesting something, and they all started to take notice of her – who is she? That started a wonderful connection. Now she loves to come and speak and bring evidence now from the people in the spirit world through Stewart's trance.

Towards the end of the evening Christopher came and having passed on messages from several people connected to Tom's old circle in 1940s, he did a 'book test' for us.

He described the cover of a book with marks on it and a fold across the middle, and told Tom he was to look at page 14. When we got home Tom went to his bookshelf and soon found this small booklet which had been his since a boy. He had carried it with him when attending the Lyceum and had folded it to fit into his jacket pocket. And of course being a child he had scribbled on the cover filling in the O's.

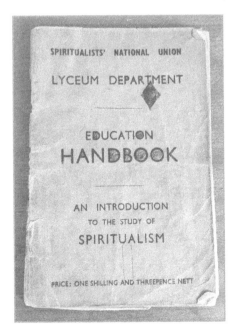

When he opened it this is what he read:

The SNU Lyceum Handbook described by Christoher.

"One of the most striking features of regularly held Home Circles is the unfailing punctuality of the Spirit guests. They never forget their appointment with us. Spirit return then is so natural that it has always happened and always will happen, so long as love and friendship are found in the universe. Just so long will those who have crossed the bridge of death into Spirit life desire to prove that love and friendship are of the Spirit and can never die."

I don't think Tom had looked at that book for years, but they obviously knew he still had it. It was a wonderful reminder how important it is to be there, because they are going to be there. Unless of course you have had to make a previous arrangement they are going to be there with you. It felt like a compliment to us for being there and being in harmony.

A Task and the Reward

Three weeks later Walter set us a task. He needed a table with a diffused red light so that they could do similar experiments to those they had done at Lime Street, Boston Massachusetts. He had obviously inspected the table which was in the centre of the circle in Hull because he knew it was hollow underneath, and if you turned it over it formed a 'well' as he put it. This wooden coffee table had a loose glass top set into a recess. He instructed Michael and Ray (and Tom to listen to this) to imagine reforming the table so that a light could be fitted below the glass on the top. Then they could have an opaque red light that would give an even glow across the surface. As Tom wasn't there that night it resulting in me asking most of the questions and making suggestions as to what was wanted.

I took the table home and between us we were able to take the legs off, turn the top over and fix the legs back on. Now the well was facing up. A small hole was made for the electric wire to go through. We fitted a light holder inside and then the glass sat on the top of the upturned base, held in place by the top lips of the four legs.

I covered the glass with three layers of red sticky 'Contact' film but it wasn't dim or diffuse enough. When we took it back to the circle, Ray covered the top with heavy red furnishing material, taped it round with thick gaffer tape and fixed a dimmer mechanism to the wire. A 'skirt' was added, to cut out the glow from where the wire went through. That table is still in use twenty seven years later. I am so pleased that my father taught me a little about joinery.

It was a privilege to do something like that for the circle and it worked, but it was a year before I was able to experience the experiment that Walter wished to do. Other people had experienced it and then one night Walter said he wanted to do something for me.

He asked me to go and sit at the table opposite Stewart. The red light was on very, very dim and against it I saw this dark mass start to move out across the red surface – a silhouette moving very slowly, stretching, a bit like a puddle of water spreading slowly on a slight slope. Slowly fingers started to appear in this mass as it pushed the ectoplasm to form around a hand. Watching it, I thought it is the same large hand I've seen before. Walter asked me to put my right hand on the table, close to the edge and just keep it there, flat. As this mass and the fingers moved towards my fingers he said:

"Here we are Ma'am, hand to hand. I want you to move your hand very slowly over the top of mine."

Ann. I'm lifting it very slightly from the table. Oh gosh .. wonderful. Right on the top Walter?

Walter. On the top ma'am.

Very slowly I moved my fingers on to his hand. I could feel the knuckles in the ectoplasmic fingers, As I moved up the back of his hand I could feel the tendons. I could even feel the hair on the back of the hand. It was so, so precise – so beautiful, soft – strong and warm.

Ann. I can feel the knuckles. Oh! A strong hand. Oh, that's wonderful, Walter!

Walter. Now isn't that not normal, is that not natural?

Ann. Oh absolutely natural.

Walter. Turn your hand to a side, ma'am.

Ann. To the side ? Over? Ohhh!

As I took my hand off his and turned it over, he grabbed it and shook it gently.

Walter. Ma'am you are the first person in your world for many years to shake the hand of Walter Stinson.

Ann. That was brilliant. It really was.

Michael. That will go down in the record books.

Ann. It was so strong and an absolutely normal, natural hand.

Walter. I am normal! (*Ann.*. You are.) (*Tom laughs*) Though some may disagree.

Ann. When we talk about how soft the ectoplasm is like a gown and Tom says it is so fine and soft, here it was absolutely natural, like human flesh. (*Tom.* That's right.) This was brilliant. Oh! Thank you."

And having been let go, I sat back in my chair. – wonderstruck.

Walter spoke again "We have not finished yet. Move your chair so you are more directly opposite Stewart and place your hand on the table." Then very quietly he said to me "You and I have a mind-to-mind communication. We understand each other." I said "Yes. We do."

Ray added "It's a handship – a friendship – handship."

Again (on the tape recording) we heard electronic interference as the ectoplasm was extruded.

As I watched the table top, a larger mass of ectoplasm came on to it and two hands were formed in that mass. They moved across the table and they gripped my hand between them. They then let go and the mass moved back.

Thanking Walter, I sat back. Walter asked Ray to turn the light down even dimmer for what he was about to do. As Ray adjusted the light Walter asked me to put my hand back on the table and requested us to keep talking, as we had all fallen silent absorbing what had just happened. Our chatter was necessary to keep the energy going for the work and Tom seemed to lead the comments saying "We are watching, waiting. We are enthralled. Wondering what's going to happen next" (*Ray.* It's exciting, yes.)

I saw a mass of ectoplasm coming up at the side to the right of Stewart. As I said "There's another large mass above. Do you know ..." my hand was lifted up between two hands, even higher and I felt a kiss on the back of them, at the base of my thumb.

I had seen the faint shape of a head leaning forward in the dimness, and at that point June said "I was going to say it looked like a head, and you know, I could see part of the shoulder and the neck, the head."

Tom. That was a kiss! Tremendous!

Denise. That was fantastic Walter! (*Tom.* It really was.)

I nearly collapsed – what a wonderful, beautiful feeling, and as Walter withdrew he said "We know at present it is all so very cr....... The tape ran out!!!

I think what he said was it was "all very crude." It wasn't as refined as they wanted it to be but they were making steps to do this wonderful experiment for people who trusted them and whom they could trust and I was so honoured to be one of those that they could try various things with.

He did stress that I was to remember all that happened for the future!

How could I ever forget that kiss by spirit, so warm and firm and real.

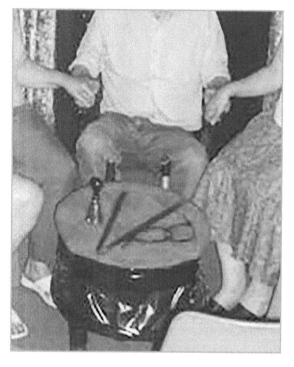

The circle is ready is to start with the table in the centre.

A New Twist on an Old Experiment

One of the experiments that the investigators had set up with "Margery" in the1920s was a sealed box containing a telegraphing mechanism. Through this Walter had been able to transmit names and short messages.

A keen fan of Stewart's circle had been researching this, and came up with the idea of a similar experiment that could be done with the 1990s' technology. He proposed the use of a karaoke machine linked to a microphone in a sealed box. It was anticipated that a spirit voice could speak into the microphone and it be heard, amplified (and recorded) by the karaoke machine.

Walter refused to go back over old ground – there were new avenues to follow, but he did agree we could give it a try by fitting a microphone in a box which had a small opening in the front. Too small for a hand to go in and it was to be placed on the floor, at the cabinet entrance to the left of Stewart, with the microphone lead passing along the wall to the machine on a shelf above Ray.

The work again fell to Tom and me – being retired we had the time to be able to do it.

Over the weeks we were aware of faint voices trying to speak to us and then one night in late July '97 at the start of the circle we heard constant tapping coming through the machine and then a growly sound as though someone was trying to speak. Slowly this became clearer and we heard a deep calm voice speaking to us.

"Are you able to hear my words?"

And a short time later "I would be grateful if you would continue to play the music."

Ray adjusted the volume, "Is that alright for you my friend?"

Voice. That is fine. I say can you hear my voice?

We replied that we could and after a few moments we heard. "Let me hear your voices."

We had been very quiet as we were trying to listen over the music and told him so to which he replied "Only when of course I am not speaking myself". He repeated this more loudly.

June. We understand.

As we listened the voice seemed to be coming from low down beside Stewart and the Voice replied "We are endeavouring to speak into the microphone. Will you try and increase the volume."

As Ray attempted to increase the microphone's volume we heard, "The young lady who is sitting to the medium's left, can you remove the trumpets."

Denise. Ok, friend. – (All three were removed)

Voice. That is much more suitable and tell me, can you hear my voice. (*All.* Yes, that's wonderful.) I am speaking through a voice box that has been created directly within this box into the microphone. I am uncertain how long I can continue to converse with you but I am doing all that is within my power to try and ... (*All.* You are doing very well – good.) You are all aware that at present we are merely experimenting to see what can be done here (*Ray.* We do understand.) because from time to time .... for us to ask for certain modifications to what you have presented us with. (*Ray.* We shall do our best.) ... As sir, you always do. (*Various circle*: It's good isn't it.) ...We had hoped to be able to speak at some length but the energy is not what we had hoped the circle as you know is not quite complete and it does have an effect on us (*Ray.* Yes we know that.) Still we are doing your best with what we have (*June.* You always do, don't you?) You will I hope notice that of late that our work has begun to progress in a slightly different direction to that which you have been used to. Whether this is apparent to you, but I will tell you this is so. There may be occasions in the near future when you may be inclined to think that nothing is happening but we are I tell you working in this slightly different way with this different kind of experiment hoping that we can refine what we are doing now.

Ray. We are quite happy to go along with you. We are very patient.

Within a few moments we heard more tapping on the microphone. This time it seemed more rhythmic. This was shortly followed by a voice saying, "Darling, Darling, it's Norman. It's Norman."

Ray exclaimed "It's Norman. Hello – come on then, Norman."

Ann. Come on then. You are doing well.

Ray. This is wonderful, Norman.

We start to hear rhythmic tapping in the microphone.

- - - .. - - - .. - - - ... - - - - - - - - - - .. - - -

Ray. You've done it once, you can do it again.

This was followed by lots more taps.

Ray. I don't understand the morse code.

Ann. Are you trying to tap out our tune?

The tapping continued in rhythm as he went through the verses.

Ray. He's tapping something out.

Ann. Well done, you!

Ray. Very good, yes we can hear you.

Ann. Just.

Norman. Darling ... I just wanted to say ... did you understand, ... did you understand?

Ann. That was our .. (*Norman.* Yes.) I thought it was (*Ann laughed*) 'I just called to say I love you.' I thought it was.

He continued tapping it out until he sealed off with a loud kissing sound.

Ray. Lovely. That was very good that. Well done, Norman.

The story of 'Our Song' went back ten years to March '87 when on a ferry from Cyprus to Haifa in Israel we were in the lounge after dinner and this "pop" band struck up. We loved dancing and so were soon on the floor doing our best with this uneven tempo and moving floor. One tune – unknown to us – was struck up and part way through, when the key changed, the singer made a 'swoop' up to the 'required' note and continued. Over the heavy sound of the engine we had no idea of the words, but laughing, continued to move to the sound of the music.

The following evening having made friends with a Norwegian couple during the day on shore in Bethlehem and Jerusalem we invited them to join us in the lounge – and on the floor when the band struck up again. As we danced to the song we had heard the night before, at the key change Norman imitated the change in key by a 'wolf howl', which resulted in us all almost collapsing with laughter.

In the din of the engines no one else would have known what the hilarity was – thank goodness.

It was almost nine months later that we finally heard the words of the Stevie Wonder song "I just called to say I love you." on the radio. How applicable and that year he sent me a card of a teddy bear on the phone –

and inside it said

Our Song – what else would he send from spirit as loving evidence.

Matter-thru-Matter

This next incredible event is something that the spirit team have really worked hard at perfecting, being sure that they can do it when you have 90 to 100 people sitting in a séance of 'friends'. When the energy is right with Stewart sitting in the cabinet, they can call up a guest to come and sit beside Stewart to witness the experience of the passage of matter-thru-matter, as have been recorded in Katie Halliwell's books about Stewart's mediumship..

One night in early 1997 Walter asked me to change places with June to sit beside Stewart. Walter again stressed that I was to remember what happened in the next few minutes – for the future. He would not say why, but that it was important.

He asked me to hold Stewart's right hand with my left hand. Stewart's arms were fastened tightly to the arms of his chair with very thick cable ties. The arm of the chair is joined at one end to the back of the chair and at the other by an upright attached to the seat so there is no possibility that the cable tie could slide off in any way, once it is fastened it is on and secure. Walter asked me to gently feel the strap which was around Stewart's wrist. It was quite tight around the arm and "be very gentle as he is in a heightened state of sensitivity."

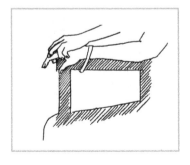

The strap was tightly in place and, as instructed, I placed my right hand back into Tom's hand on the other side of me.

Drawing by Katie Halliwell of the starting position of the hands and cable tie for the experiment.

I felt Stewart's arm start to pull up and down, up and down, pulling against the arm of the chair. Suddenly his arm was up in the air taking my arm with it. (I was holding on to his hand so naturally my arm was up in the air.) Walter asked me to feel the arm of the chair "Is the strap still there?" Yes, it was and I pulled against so everyone could hear the sound of it. It was still solid. I heard a slight noise and slowly down came our arms.

Walter asked me to feel Stewart's arm again. "Is the strap in place?"

With my right hand, I reached across and felt Stewart's wrist and arm. "No, it's not there."

"Check again."

"No, it's definitely not around his arm."

I heard a slight indefinable noise and Walter said "Check again." The strap was back around Stewart's arm, fastening it to the chair.

Within a split second our arms were up in the air again. Under instruction, I checked the chair again feeling to the very back. There was no strap. It was not there – "Check again!" I did – definitely no cable tie.

Our arms came slowly down to rest on the arm of the chair and with that, as our arms came to rest, I felt a large hand on the top of mine – I was still holding Stewart's hand. With his left arm still fastened to the opposite arm of the chair, here was another hand – on top of mine – and under it was a closed cable tie. But the moment I felt it there, under the hand, it was around my wrist and within a second it had gone through.

It had gone through my arm!

I felt it, and I still feel the sensation as I write this. A closed tie passing through my flesh! I was amazed. How did they do that? I know I didn't imagine it. In fact I have had to listen to the recording again and I definitely said, "It's gone through!"

"Ann, check Stewart's arm." – There was no strap.

"Check again, right up the arm." This time I felt right up to his elbow. Not a sign of it. It was not there. Walter then said, "Keep your right hand on Stewart's wrist."

Imagine this, his arm is resting on the chair, my left hand is holding Stewart's right hand and the fingers of my right hand are resting on his wrist where the strap should be – and as they rested there, I felt the strap come back – passing through the tips of my fingers as they rested on his arm.

I felt the strap around his arm and *immediately* the strap was removed again. I felt it disappear from under my fingers and it was given to me – still locked – as a memento. Very, very special.

It is kept in my special box. It is only something small – some will say you can make a new one any time, but for me it is the memory that it holds – and to have the recording as well – makes the memory even more special.

Walter asked Ray if there was a new strap available on the table and he fastened a new strap around Stewart's arm. I felt it as it passed my sleeve and I heard the 'Brrr' as the end passed over the teeth.

Walter told me to leave go of Stewart's hand and as I did so someone ruffled my hair and tapped the back of my hand. Walter said "There will come a time when that experiment you will remember well. That is a puzzle. Something you will not lose sight of again."

"Thank you, Walter."

It was all vividly brought back to me in January 2021 (24 years later) – not that I'd ever forgotten the sensation of the strap passing through my arm. When setting up Katie Halliwell's new book, '*Touching the Next Horizon*' I came across the passage where Walter explained to Leslie Kean (author of *Surviving Death*) about the difference in the energies used in the circle.

Leslie was told that matter-thru-matter needs a very different kind of energy from ectoplasm and it calls for a special kind of energy from the medium.

Katie was also there that night and wrote this:

> "He told us that when the living matter through matter demonstration takes place, the spirit people extract from the medium a unique form of energy which is not to be confused with

ectoplasmic energy. When the interlink takes place, Stewart's right arm and the arm of the lady who is holding the medium's hand exist not within the physical world nor within the spiritual, but between the two. When these limbs, existing now between the two worlds, are lifted into the air that is the precise moment when the procedure is complete and that causes the sound. It is like a snapping sound. When they lower their arms back to the chair, there is no resistance, for there is nothing physical and Stewart's arm returns through the looped strap left hanging on the chair arm.

Throughout all those years of sitting, we in the circle thought the snapping sound was caused by the strap, but it is not so, it is the coming together of the spiritual and physical energies. When the strap is being presented to the lady as a memento, the two energies gradually begin to move apart and after the spirit people have re-secured Stewart the arms become wholly 'physical' once more."

So at that point, being linked with Stewart, my arm – if not all of me – was 'between the two worlds', my arm was no longer fully physical and it could join in. Was it then my 'etheric' body that had experienced the effect of the strap passing through it not my dense physical body? If for those few seconds my arm had no longer been 'solid' it seems it was possible – What a sensation and what a privilege.

Was this explanation to Leslie the reason Walter had said 'There will come a time when that experiment you will remember well.'?

It's wonderful to know that you can be so close, that you can have that experience happen; that you can be so trusted and loved that they can do that with you. It is such an honour, it really is.

An Ectoplasm Experience

One evening in the summer of 1998 there were only three of us sitting with Stewart. This time it was Stewart's brother Michael, Tom and myself. There had recently been a programme on the television about the medium Helen Duncan. When she was accused of swallowing and then regurgitating cheesecloth to replicate a materialised figure. The discussion prior to the sitting had jokingly been all about the ectoplasm – 'It's cheesecloth' – 'No it's crinkly cellophane' – 'No it's cheesecloth'.

That night I was able to sit next to Stewart, as his sister Gaynor was away and Michael was in charge of the light, the music and the recorder. We had already had several spirit visitors when Freda came and asked us to try the red light under the surface of the table so that they could try out the brightness that the ectoplasm could withstand that night. As the ectoplasm was extracted, via Stewart's navel we were told, we could hear it fizzing and crackling. I said, "There you are it's crinkly cellophane." and Michael again re-joined, "It's cheesecloth!" Tom told us that the sound was just as he remembered fifty years before.

That evening, under Freda's instructions, we were able to turn the light up higher than ever before and see the amorphous shape of

the ectoplasm silhouetted against the light of the table top. It then formed into a pincer, with which a 'trumpet' or other objects could have been picked up.

Katie's drawing of the ectoplasmic 'pincer', which she witnessed preparing to write.

Freda then told us to turn the light out and moments later said, "Ann, put out your hand, palm up."

I held out my right hand towards Stewart. My wrist was grasped by strong fingers so that I could not move it out of the position they wanted. Stewart, as usual, was fastened into his chair with ropes, and his arms secured to the arms of his chair with strong cable ties so it could not have been his hand grasping my wrist. I felt something moving across my fingers. In texture it was like a small plastic bag full of liquid, a cool soft bag, fluid, but not crinkly but that sort of material. I tried to dsecribe it to the others.

The 'bag' was moved up and down across my fingers and then suddenly it was gone, and my wrist was released.

I heard Freda say, "Put your hand down."

I put my hand down and sat quietly.

"Ann put your hand out."

I put it out again; again it was grasped at the wrist and this time across my palm came a piece of roughish cloth – a bit like a bandage. I could feel this cloth being pulled across my hand. I tried to describe it. "It's like a piece of cloth."

Quickly came back Freda's brusque words, "Like cheesecloth!"

It was quite different from fabric previously when I had felt it so soft, silky – like voile.

As quickly as it had come it had gone and I could lower my hand.

Freda spoke again, "Then let us try what I suppose is in the dematerialised state. That is to say before it takes on solid form. Give me your hand again, Ann, and you must tell everyone here what you can feel. It you are able to feel anything. I am taking your hand with my other hand."

This time, as fingers went round my wrist, other fingers held the tips of my fingers so that my hand was absolutely still, just below Stewart's mouth. There was a slight regurgitating sound from Stewart, and across my hand came a cool draught. It was nothing like someone blowing on your hand, more like the cold air that flows on to you when you open a large freezer. That was the feeling, but so, so gentle. Slowly I became aware that it was less cool and slowing – stopping. My fingers were released, and I lowered my arm.

They had given me the chance to feel what ectoplasm could be like – what they could do with it. I knew what it was like as flesh, when Walter had invited me to feel the back of his hand, when he had materialised it against the under-lit table, so I knew what it was like materialised—and now I had experienced it before it was formed, when it first comes out – and in other states too.

In some of the photographs there is a gap between the medium's mouth and the object, that's the ectoplasm that's flowing. That's before it becomes physical, before the scientists work on it to make it into what they need – whether they need it to be a steel rod, or a gown, or a face, or hair or beards. Tom had experienced beards back in the1940s, feeling the beards of his Grandfather and his Lyceum leader, Mr Roeder, in his mother's circle.

Just to have these wonderful experiences I know were given to me because I would be able to pass on the knowledge and experience of what spirit can do when a medium – a group will sit in dedication – and it does take dedication.

Two years later, in a private sitting, Freda gave Katie Halliwell this description of what ectoplasm is:

"Life itself is a trinity. There is the physical, there is the spiritual body and then there is the mind. The physical body is that which you inhabit as you proceed along through life upon the earthly path. But the life of the physical body is merely temporary... but your spiritual body is an exact replica of your physical body.

Within your spiritual body is your mind – the mind is all that you are; all that you were and all that you will be. It is your personality; it is your complete memory. It is you in totality, but it is the eternal aspect of yourself for your spiritual body together with your mind will proceed on into eternity. It is indestructible, dear. Your physical brain is merely an instrument of the mind that is all.

It is nothing in itself but it gives physical expression to your mind, dear, the eternal aspect of yourself. You will therefore understand that there is physical matter and there is spiritual matter. Between the two is a form of dynamic energy which we often refer to as ectoplasm for it is neither physical nor spiritual in nature; it is the only substance or energy which lies between the two states of existence. It is both spiritual and it is physical.

When you take part in a physical séance and we attempt to manifest in a physical manner we must take from the medium the energy, the vital energy, the substance, ectoplasm, and it is upon this that all physical phenomena rests and depends; without that there would be no physical contacts. It is between the two states of existence, unique to neither but common to both.

Ectoplasm can be manipulated by the scientific people in my world in such a manner that its very nature can be changed. Its molecular structure can be changed from something that is almost smoke–like in appearance to something which is solid to the touch.

It can be changed; it can be manipulated to something which is filmy, which is unsubstantial to something which is very substantial, that is solid to the touch. From the ectoplasm the scientific people are able to create what we often refer to as either pseudopods or ectoplasmic arms it is these that are connecting themselves to the trumpets, but the other end of the arm or the pseudopod must remain in contact with the medium for it is truly a part of the medium. It is a vital form of energy.

We are then able to change the structure of the arm from something which is invisible to something, on occasions, which is visible and it is this which will support and manipulate the trumpets.

Ectoplasm is extremely sensitive to any form of light – it is rather like the photographer trying to develop his photographs in light – it cannot be done. It has to be done the whole process within the darkroom. Life itself cannot be generated within light. It generates within darkness, within the womb of the mother, and it is like an accelerated form of life itself. It is the birth of this form of energy but takes nine months to reach fruition is created in seconds within the séance room. If suddenly light is introduced within the séance room, then the ectoplasm would return extremely quickly to the medium and this could create a haemorrhage, That is why it is dangerous. Physical mediumship, the exercising of physical mediumship is always dangerous. It has the danger – it has danger connected with it at all times and for precisely that reason most of the physical mediums in the past have chosen to work within the safety of their own séance rooms."

Ambitious Plans

The spirit team had ambitious plans for the Circle in Hull. In the work that they were being able to do they could see that very soon they could, maybe, have materialisation in light.

Tom was asked to write reports for the Noah's Ark Newsletter which would encourage other groups to keep going – after all, Stewart had been sitting for 25 years before the 'explosion' of phenomena we had witnessed over the previous few years.

This was his first report in February 1999 which gives a clear example of the variety of phenomena we had on many an evening. Though there were other evenings when nothing much might seem to happen, when the 'team' were busy working in the background.

Circle Report, 15th February 1999

We all considered that the sitting on 15th February 1999 was very significant – both from the special feeling of tranquillity and peacefulness in the room and the physical phenomena we were so privileged to experience that night. It was not one of our longest sittings – about an hour – but so much happened, so quickly that my record of it may not be sequentially correct – but here goes.

Stewart was quickly in trance – a matter of a few minutes – and from the very beginning we heard tappings on the microphone which stands close to his left shoulder. At the same time there were lots of taps from various parts of the room. June and Gaynor both 'felt' spirit presences near them at the front of the cabinet curtains. The curtains were frequently closed and opened again by our spirit helpers and at times were draped across June's and Gaynor's knees. Within a few minutes June had one of the cushions from an empty chair on the other side of the room dropped on to her lap, and later the two drumsticks from the table were also put on to her lap.

Walter Stinson was soon speaking to us – very clearly – but his voice was coming from about six feet in the air in front of the cabinet instead of from Stewart's mouth as usual. He explained that he was using an independent voice box – from a 'crudely' (his word) materialised body. He immediately asked us all to move our chairs back towards the walls and remove the table which is normally standing in the centre of the circle group.

Tom had felt a tap on his left knee early in the sitting but after Walter had spoken to us Tom then felt the shape of a large hand slapping and then gripping his left knee. All the sitters could hear the slapping and Gaynor asked if the hand was solid. The response from Walter was immediate and we all heard a distinct clapping of two hands in front of Gaynor. Soon after Walter started speaking, we heard loud 'shuffling' of feet in the space we had made, and he told us it was himself in the early stages of full materialisation. We were obviously very excited and he told us that everyone in 'his' world was just as excited at the progress being made this year! He assured us that as soon as the forms were suitable, they would be considering the use of light in the room.

This would be the 'icing on the cake'.

During all these happenings, June felt her hair being played with, and behind Tom's head there were numerous 'clickings' – heard by all in the room. Everyone felt the coldness below the knees and we were told that this was because the centre of energy was low down in the room. Then June and Tom heard a spirit form moving in front of them and actually felt the breath on their faces. Tom then felt his hair being played with, followed by stroking on his left cheek and finally a gentle 'tweaking' of his left ear. He felt it was his mother, Minnie, but at that time could not be sure of course. Irrespective of that, he said it was a very moving moment, reminiscent of their Home Circle over 50 years ago.

After Minnie had gone we heard Walter saying quite clearly – "Go on then, try it for yourself", after which we heard smaller feet shuffling in front of the cabinet – which we learned later were Christopher's – but he had only been able to build his legs and feet, unlike Walter and Minnie who had built the complete bodies in a crude form. About this time Walter told us it was about time to close and that Stewart would take a little longer to come out of trance this week and not to call him as we usually did. We then heard heavy breathing and thought it would be White Feather to give his closing blessing – but we were wrong and were surprised to hear Freda speaking for a few minutes. She confirmed that it was Tom's mother who had worked very hard to materialise, with the help of Tom's father, Tosher, and it was a unique experience for her as she had been the medium during their Home Circle to enable so many hundreds of spirits to materialise all those years ago. Freda also spoke to Tom and said that the special feeling we had experienced at the beginning of the sitting was that unique feeling for materialisation phenomena which Tom had experienced in their Home Circle. She then told us that some weeks there may be very little or even nothing happening when they were concentrating on materialisation and then we were to close after half an hour.

Just before she left, Freda asked Tom who was Gladys – at which moment Tom had felt as though a spirit presence had almost pushed him from the front. Freda said Gladys was a strong-minded person (which Tom confirmed) – and she had actually 'lunged' towards him. Freda then told us to close immediately. After the closing prayer Stewart slowly came out of trance, telling us that he knew someone had been as his jaw was aching again.

An extremely active and remarkable sitting enhanced by the encouragement from Walter all the work and development over the years to achieve full materialisations in light could come to fruition THIS YEAR. We all left that room 'walking on air'!

Tom Harrison

After the sitting Tom told us that the Gladys who had made her presence known was in fact Gladys Owen, who was a very strong-minded person, and whom he had known well from the late 1960s while he was the Manager of the Arthur Findlay College, at Stansted Hall.

Eleven months later Tom, at the request of Freda, wrote another Report for the 'Ark'

As regular members of Stewart Alexander's Home Circle for a number of years, we have been very privileged to witness some remarkable physical phenomena and at our last sitting we were asked by one of Stewart's main communicators, Freda Johnson, to write a brief article to encourage all the other dedicated Home Circles to witness some remarkable physical phenomena and at our last sitting we were asked by one of Stewart's main communicators, Freda Johnson, to write a brief article to encourage all the other dedicated Home Circles to continue with their search for the Truth of our Continuous Existence and the great joy of Spirit Communion.

At the beginning of last year Walter Stinson and his vast team of spirit workers set themselves a target to produce fully materialised spirit people walking around the room in a light, by the end of the year. In our ignorance we assumed he was referring to the normal red light used in many Circles – as in my own mother's Circle some 50 years ago – but during our last sitting in 1999 they had quite a surprise for us. Stewart was roped in his chair as always, with his wrists fixed to the chair arms by means of the usual cable tie strapping. After the initial opening chat with Walter he asked us to move our chairs back to the walls of the room and clear the centre of the floor. Stewart's sister Gaynor was in her usual seat on Stewart's left with June on his right and they were asked to keep close contact with Stewart.

The cabinet curtains were closed by our spirit friends and when they opened them we could all clearly see this very bright ball of light emanating from where Stewart was sitting. It was a wonderful experience to witness it then travelling around the room many feet from the cabinet. This continued for some time with the size of the ball growing to about four inches. It then stopped in front of Gaynor and she became so excited, telling us that she could see a lady's face in the ball of light! They had outwitted us by bringing their own light to show the face of a spirit lady.

The light continued to emanate for a few more minutes before the cabinet curtains were closed again by our Spirit friends. Walter then spoke and after the curtains had been re-opened he asked Gaynor to place her right hand on Stewart's strapped left hand on the chair arm – which she did. After a few moments she said she could feel 'somebody' standing in front of her, between herself and Stewart, and then we all heard the footsteps loud and clear of the Spirit person walking around the room. They then spoke to us from a position in the centre of the room whilst Stewart was still strapped to his chair, as confirmed by Gaynor who was still holding his hand on the chair arm.

I was sitting next to June with my chair backed on to the wall, about seven feet from the cabinet and my hands resting on my knees. Quite suddenly I felt two large, warm hands grasp my right hand, pat it loudly and then give me a strong handshake! I checked with Gaynor that she was still holding Stewart's hand, which she confirmed. During the walk around the room, Ann, who was sitting next to me, felt two large hands gently placed on her head – as did Gaynor later. The presence of this very solid spirit person in the room lasted for 4 to 5 minutes, and as their visit was coming to a close, we heard the voice in the centre of the room again telling us that they had hoped to have a red light also but the power had not been quite sufficient. As they were speaking, we heard the voice gradually sinking towards the floor saying they could not hold the weight any longer which brought back deep-seated memories of similar happenings in my mother's circle when someone materialised for the first time.

Ann and I were particularly privileged and pleased to have these experiences just prior to our move to Spain. Freda assured us that they would still be around us doing our work there and they looked forward to meeting again in Stewart's Circle during our visits to the U.K.

The major purpose of this brief report is give encouragement to those hundreds of dedicated sitters who may feel they are 'getting nowhere'. This type of physical phenomena does not happen overnight – far from it – as our good friend Colin Fry will also confirm. So be of good heart and know that even if you are not blessed with such rare and special phenomena, the fact that you are sitting in communion with your loved ones and friends in the Spirit World is a great joy to be cherished. Yes, we shall certainly miss our weekly sittings in Stewart's Circle – but Life moves on and we have been told that our move is 'for the greater good'. There is much spirit activity in the area we are moving to, and we hope to be able to add our 'twopenn'orth' in a positive manner.

Tom Harrison 11.1.00

Our Home Circle and Rescues

In the time that Tom and I were together at my home near Ferriby in East Yorkshire we sat, just the two of us, to make and keep contact with our friends, family and various spirits who wanted to work with us or needed help.

We tried sitting with a small table but on that first evening Tom was told (mentally) just to sit. We did, and very quickly I felt I was an ancient Celtish fighter, hiding among the roots of a large tree in dense woodland, and with that I felt a strong blow on the back of my head. I continued to watch....

In a way it was like watching a movie, but I soon realised I was being shown I was needed to 'rescue' this ancient warrior. To help him move on from hiding, to know he had died and there was more to be experienced. I told Tom what I felt and could see and gradually he encouraged the warrior to look towards a distant light which he could see and that it was safe to move towards it. I can't say that I felt any difference at first but eventually I felt at peace. That was my first experience of doing a "rescue".

It wasn't to be the last.

A year later when we had moved to a new home some miles away, but still in Yorkshire, we were contacted, through a friend, by a couple who had a 'mysterious' photograph taken by a friend of their foster son. This photo had been taken on the young man's day out with friends at a youth centre which had been a church. It showed a clear image of a man in Norman style chain mail with his head back as though he had been attacked from behind. It was a clear instance of a "spirit" photograph. They had had the photograph examined at a photographic dept of a local University that had found no indication it was a double exposure.

When they visited us, having heard their story, we decided to sit with the Ouija board. We were used to using it and had had good information through it. Having opened with a prayer we very quickly had this information: SAXON – SON OF GODWIN, RAKANHAG. (The name was given twice when I questioned the spelling.)[1] It then spelled out that he would come back.

Psychic / spirit photograph taken by an amateur
photographer somewhere in South Yorkshire 1997.[2]

The following Friday, our normal night for sitting, the board spelled out that – he was a Hall man, in bond to the Manor Hall at Wolwick. ...'NORMANS TOOK THE HALL – LORD HAD NO QUARREL WITH THEM.' We still had no idea who was giving us this information.

Two weeks later, after thinking about this brave man who was obviously stuck between 'lives', when sitting with the board again the name VERONICA was spelt out gently and slowly. This followed:

"WISH TO TELL YOU ABOUT RAKANHAG... HE WAS GOOD MAN ... IN OUR HOUSE (I asked 'Were you the Lord's daughter') NO. WIFE. TELL THEM BACK STABBER. (He was killed by someone in your household) YES. WE ALL KILLED."

---

1. The name was given to us in 1998. Long before the advent of computer games which I have just learned about in trying to find the origins of the name.
2. Rotate image to view the superimposed spirit form more clearly.

We discovered that the manor was nowhere near the church in the photo, nor near the lad's home. I asked, "Have you been able to help Rakanhag?" "HE KNOWS NOW. WE ALL WORK WITH HIM TO HELP YOU. I WAS TAKEN TO WATCH RAKANHAG'S RESCUE."

Can you remember your family name? PERCY.

Veronica was unable to recall her husband's name – she didn't want to. We also learned later that when it spelled out 'We all killed' it had meant that they all knew of the plot, not that they were all killed.

At this point Tom was controlled by Rakanhag. His head went back in anguish, and could only grunt "Thank you" when I invited him to come through again. Sunrise then controlled the planchette and told us he was helping him and that Rakanhag wished to work with us and protect us.

After this I frequently felt him close – particularly by a sharp pain in my left ribs at the back (where he had been stabbed?). Through Tom's trance Sunrise told us that he had felt his death again "for a moment." When I asked if it would get better over time, he told us it would. Sunrise also told us that Rakanhag was working with him, and for several months came to protect the circle, as our 'Door keeper' whenever we sat, and that he would for as long as he was needed, before he moved on to do other work. The following week as we started the circle Rakanhag was immediately there, causing Tom to arch back in his chair, his arms twitching at his side until he overcame the "death throes" again. Then "he" sat forward and grasped my hand and then Carole's. There was great strength and powerful energy with him. A wonderful protector for us.

One evening at a friends' circle when we were sitting for table movement he (Rakanhag) became startled by this 'strange' movement of a table and drew close to protect me. I felt the knife in my ribs and his power with me. I had to reassure him, mentally, that everything was all right and I was safe.

It was more than a year later when we were sitting for Tom's trance development that Tom suddenly stood, appeared to grow very tall and stretched up his arms saying loudly "FREE, FREE. Doing much work now – always with you to guard." Tom continued to stand rigidly to 'attention' as though on guard. Rakanhag had returned to tell us he had learned that he was no longer a "bound" man – but was free and able to move on – to progress, and learning to do healing work under Sunrise's guidance. Having thanked us for helping him he left, and Tom relaxed and resumed his seat, still under trance control.

After that I no longer felt that stab in the ribs when he drew near and I am so happy that we had been able to help a 'stuck' soul move on.

This may seem far-fetched but I assure you it did happen – I still have the notes we made at the time and I know we couldn't have made up the story.

The two of us had sat together regularly for over a year before we made contact with Carole, our tutor at a Counselling course we signed up for in order to help people who came for healing. She was very psychic and often communicated with her horses. A true spirit. She slotted in well and we took it in turns to try to develop our trance and transfiguration capabilities.

As Tom's trance and transfiguration developed. Carole, Tom and I sat close together in a dim red light, and weekly saw faces develop and change as Tom sat. We continued to start each evening with the Ouija board and one evening the planchette moved in a figure of eight but sideways – the infinity sign, this was followed by FATTER. The symbol as repeated but this time it was also fatter.

Can you tell us your name? W N... W N... WINSTON – followed by ∞ again.

Do you have a surname?   OF COURSE... S-C... S-C.

It doesn't matter, does it?   NO

You have joined us recently?   YES.

You are coming to try to work?   NO

Sorry. You are coming to work?   YES.

Coming to work with Tom?   YES.

Later that same evening as we sat for Tom's trance development someone controlling him motioned us to watch his face by circling his hand around it. He did not speak because of the energy and

86

Winston S. Churchill
(taken by Karsh of Ottowa)

concentration needed to mould the face. He showed himself as a younger man. As we watched, the neck seemed to thicken, and deep lines appeared at the sides of the top lip – as we would know him in later years. He 'raised his hat' in a characteristic way and waved his right hand in a slightly 'royal' manner. Carole didn't recognise him but I did – it was W.S.C. – Winston Spencer Churchill. As we talked over the sitting later Tom told us he felt that Churchill had been there.

That was the first of a number of contacts with him and not only through Tom.

A very special connection

The effort that was put into Tom's development would seem to be paying off when in the Autumn of 1998 Tom read of a request from a couple living on the Algarve in Portugal. They were asking for someone to go and teach their group about Spirit and communication. We decided that we could do that, and Tom replied we would be happy to do so.

Naturally, as they had no idea who we were, Frederick, the writer of the request, wanted to meet us before he accepted our offer. Over telephone conversations it was discovered that, as we were holidaying over Christmas in South Africa with Tom's son Colin and family, and they were travelling there too, the best place to meet up was in Pretoria on the 27th December, when they were on their way to Victoria Falls by train!

The journey from Johannesburg to Pretoria was delightful, with time to stop off at Gen. Jan Smuts' home, now a museum, and to walk in his garden , where Colin picked up an acorn and said "Here grow a tree." – We did, and I planted it in memory of Tom at Cober Hill in 2011 and it is flourishing (with the help of his ashes).

We arrived at the Victoria Hotel in the late afternoon and on a shady Edwardian verandah were met by a very welcoming couple, Valerie and Frederick Smith. In the course of sharing our stories Frederick placed a straw hat on the table. Tom did not know it was Frederick's son, Scott's, but the moment Tom touched it he went into a light trance and Scott communicated.

Our meeting with Frederick and Valerie in Pretoria

This is what Frederick wrote to me recently.

I remember being so amazed that someone sitting so close could link with Scott, as previous experience was with mediums on stages, far away. To have Tom sitting next to me made it seem almost unreal. Then he brought through my son, Scott and it was so unmistakably Scott that one's mind goes blank for a few minutes whilst the brain copes with something new. Having a real live legend sitting next to me and linking with Spirit was a first for me (probably ten thousandth time for Tom) and one never forgets those significant moments in one's life.

That precious moment became the beginning of a wonderful friendship, for though Tom could put anyone at ease and had no ego, I always felt so humble in his presence. What Tom experienced in his life is quite unbelievable and I still find it a tremendous privilege not only to have known him but to have had such an unscheduled sitting in the middle of Africa. What a wonderful memory.   Thanks a million, Tom.

Our offer to teach at their home in Portugal was accepted and we travelled there the following May – the first of many happy visits to stay with them.

Back in Brayton, early in 1999 we were joined by our old friends from the West Yorkshire circle. The couple no longer sat at home and missed the contact. We were only too happy to have them join us. Eventually Carole found a better job in 'caring' which involved working on a Friday, but with a family of four to take care of she could not refuse it. However, that still left us with a most harmonious circle of four.

Because we were sitting in our large lounge, we made a cabinet of sheets of MDF, and painted it matt black on the inside so that the energy could be concentrated on whoever was sitting in it. We all took it in turns each week – apart from P--- who often found himself rooted to his armchair and was happy to work from there. J--- didn't like the cabinet as she said she preferred knowing what was going on and didn't want to go into trance. As she was almost the best developed physical medium we knew we didn't push her, but she didn't like us to sing the "trigger" songs that we'd used before – until her team managed to take her into trance anyway.

They were then able to swing the trumpet about and pick up the bells and ring them, and twice, after writing a message on our pad, transported the pencil away across the room. One hiding place wasn't found for five months.

One morning following the sitting, we found that our main radiator had been turned off. It never had been off before, but Grey Wolf liked to "work in the cold," as he made a point of telling us. After that we made sure our heating was turned down and that radiator was off. So – 'No fire in the teepee' – as we were told on another occasion.

Soon we had voices speaking through the 'voice box', way up almost at ceiling height. The old 'team' of Beryl, Wilf, Jenny – the little girl, and others had joined us. One evening the trumpet was up in the air when it knocked against something solid. At first we thought it was J---'s head, as she was sitting in the cabinet, but it moved and tapped her and then tapped another solid body some feet away – and taller. It continued to tap a solid body all the way down, showing us that there was a 'person' materialised, and out in the room. It was another of their team, Abe.

Another Rescue

One evening in mid July 1999, after we had sat for Tom and Carole's development, we started to sing our normal opening Nursery Rhymes and it was not long before J--- was in trance, in the chair beside me. As always I was in charge of the red light and the recorder.

In complete darkness now for J--- , we were singing happily through our repertoire when I heard a sharp tapping on the metal stem of the tall red lamp beside me. We all responded, to acknowledge their presence. We continued to sing and I felt a strong tap on my shoulder followed by another tap on the top of the lamp. I thought that I was meant to turn the lamp on, but we didn't have any light when J--- was in trance and I said so. Again there was a very sharp poke on my shoulder and a tap on the lamp followed by the deep familiar voice of J---'s guide, Grey Wolf, "Ann – Light!"

"Sorry, Grey Wolf, I thought that was what you meant but we don't usually have light now."

I turned on the lamp, with it pointing towards the floor. In the dim light we could see that J--- was sitting hunched and unresponsive. I turned the light a little more towards her. Her face was twisted and she did not speak. I realised, intuitively, that the person with J--- was blind and dumb with no idea where she was.

I started to talk to her quietly while mentally projecting what I was saying and visualising a group of welcoming people and a warm but bright light. The rest of the circle joined in sending their healing

thoughts as they realised this person needed help to move on to a better place – to 'heaven' you might say. As I concentrated I could 'see' a beautiful warm bright light with Aunt Agg beckoning to her. It took several minutes of quiet chat before we saw J---'s body and face relax and we knew our 'friends' had her safe.

The following week we received this message on our pad and we were told that they had managed to reach her, and she was now safe. She had been not only deformed but also deaf, blind and mute so that they had been unable to contact as she couldn't understand. They knew with our help, from our 'mortal plane' she could be helped to make the journey to a better life – just as we had for the Celtish warrior and Rakanhag.

A Levitation that went wrong

It was to be a busy summer, as two weeks later we had a lot of small happenings during the sitting – taps, clunks, things were heard to move. Carole then felt someone stand on her toe, Ann felt a sudden icy-cold draught across her hand and a voice beside Tom (in the cabinet) said "Was it all right?" ... "So So." Tom and Carole felt someone standing between them and another voice said "Peace and Love. Sorry, would have put it back but not enough energy."

This was followed by J--- saying, "What am I doing down here? I'm sat on the floor."

The circle was quickly (but properly) closed and when I switched on the red light J--- was beside me on the floor and her chair was across the room by the door. She was very groggy.

The levitated chair and groggy medium

P--- quickly moved across, sat her in Carole's chair giving her healing.

It seems the 'Team' had tried to levitate her in her chair, as years before in their own home, but ran out of energy to complete it.

I decided to take a photograph of the circle space and the photo *(opposite right)* is what I got. Was this Grey Wolf's energy still there to support J--- or the residual energy from the attempted levitation?

A Pre Op. chat

In October '99 we persuaded out friend Eric to come and sit with the circle. He was due to go into hospital again for another major heart operation. He had experienced our healing but never a spiritualist physical circle. His wife Jackie was too afraid to sit with us but took a seat in my study to read while we sat.

He thoroughly enjoyed the experience but was rather perturbed by Wilf's comment. This is what Eric wrote:

".... It became obvious during the year ('99) that all was not well with my heart and a second operation was scheduled for 10th December. I visited Tom and Ann very regularly to build up the extra energy to help me through the operation. They had talked to me about their sittings with their friend the medium and her husband and felt I must join them one Saturday evening. I had always declined as I did not feel up to driving on my own in an evening, and did not want to infringe on Jackie's weekend as she worked all week. They said if she did not want to join us they would quite understand and she could bring a book and read in the study – which was what was arranged.

I did not know what to expect and when I saw the cabinet, trumpet, bells and notebook and pencil I must admit I wondered what was coming. We started with songs and carols and I joined in with gusto. Within seconds the trumpet was flying all round the room and we had a number of visitations including one of the medium's Spirit helpers, who spoke to me directly and took a long time to explain that his job was to receive new Spirits – and he assured me all would be well. I remember saying to Tom afterwards that I was concerned that the communicator had gone to such great lengths to tell me about his job as 'Spiritual receptionist' and hoped he wasn't just preparing me! This was said with tongue in cheek but the communicator assured Tom at a subsequent sitting, that he just wanted to put me at my ease and apologised – which of course I accepted."[2]

---

2. Eric's full report is in *'Life After Death: Living Proof'* (SNPP 2008)

The week before Eric came to the Saturday sitting, we had agreed, on request from one of our Spirit friends, Jenny, a delightful little girl, to put a few jelly babies in a dish for the Spirit children the following week. I therefore, put five in a dish and put them on the table in the centre of the Circle, which Eric saw before we started. As soon we opened the medium's Spirit Guide 'Grey Wolf' spoke to Eric. "Good evening Eric. I want to say before proceeding any further, you are perfectly safe, don't worry and your good lady is safe also. Now sing."

During the singing our heavy brass crinoline lady bell (the same bell as in the original circle, Gladys had given it to us as a Wedding present, see p.10) was picked up and rung above our heads, which amazed Eric. The trumpet also moved rapidly around the room before finally stopping in mid-air in front of the cabinet, pointing towards Eric. We heard a faint voice trying to speak to him and eventually heard "This is Auntie." She then spoke briefly to him.

This proved to be excellent evidence for Eric, which he later explained to us. During our previous healing sessions with him, I often felt the strong presence of a lady and from the description I gave him he recognised her as one of his relatives, 'Auntie Florrie'. She was in fact his mother's Aunt but had become very close to Eric and frequently took him on day trips. What we had not known, however, was that as the 'senior' Aunt in the family, she was known to everyone in the family simply as 'Auntie' – without the Florrie, which was only used when talking to other people, like ourselves.

Jenny, the spirit child, came again to thank me for the jelly babies and said they hadn't been able to eat them all, which rather puzzled us at the time. When the light was switched on at the end of the sitting however, there in the dish, which had had five jelly babies when we started, was only half a black one, which, from its appearance, looked as though it had been bitten through! We were all quite surprised by this – especially Eric of course, and we still have it, wrapped, in our box of memorabilia. Eric had been enjoyably perplexed by it all and was delighted to see that the Spirit Guide had printed a message for him on the pad which read: "We are with you always." This page was torn out for Eric to keep as a memento of his first sitting in a Home Circle. And his account finishes with... "This was an evening I will never forget."

We became very good friends with Eric and Jackie and did all we could to help Eric through his second, more serious, operation. It seemingly worked as Eric wrote...

"I was certainly aware of the help that Tom and Ann were giving me. Before the first operation I was terrified, but this time, although I knew what to expect, and that it would be more serious than the previous one, I was relaxed and laid back. In the event the operation was much more difficult. I was on the operating table for five and a half hours where they performed a quadruple bypass and reconstruction of an artery.

The Spirits were right – I did have a rough recovery with additional pain and numerous setbacks including a transfusion of the wrong blood. My kidneys almost failed and I was hours away from dialysis. Tom and Ann played a major part in helping me through this, visiting the hospital in Hull and I always felt a boost when I needed it most. I have to say on a very selfish note however, that I considered their move to Spain in January 2000, most inopportune! Since then we have visited each other and had weekly 'remote' healing sessions, which Tom likes to call 'energy balancing'. These have certainly helped and I have become stronger over the months. Thank you, Tom and Ann, I could not have managed without you."

The communicator who described himself as the 'Spirit Receptionist' was Wilf. A wonderful jovial spirit who had been a publican in the Birmingham area while on earth and we remembered him well from the West Yorkshire circle days. He had explained at length how he met "newcomers" to their new world. Speaking by Independent Direct Voice he said to Eric.

"I just want to say to the gentleman. Well you know, my job don't you, seeing new folks over? So I've just got to say to this gentleman – everything's all right, don't worry. All right? I look after folk who come to my side. Some don't believe, but that doesn't matter. They are all looked after and then when it's time for them they are shown the right way, Okay. So I just don't want you to worry, cos that's my job. It's different isn't it? I look after people who used to think to themselves this is all rubbish. Right? And that doesn't matter because they do realise in time that everybody has a chance. I'm nobody really. I'm just at the bottom. I just see to people when they first come over. But just a minute ... I'll tell him ... I have got a man here who belongs to you – but he's much further up than me – he's a lot more .... than I have but when he was here in your world he used to think when you're dead you're dead – but he knows different now. I want you to know this man – and Ooo he's really strong –he's going to be with you. We know all that's happening to you and don't worry cos we are there and I'll tell you summat. Well, *you'll know that we are there*. Right? I'm not going to tell you how – cos you'll know. ... I'm working hard tonight, ain't I?

Right but please don't worry because we are aware of everything that's happening. ... We understand your personal thoughts. And it's okay to talk to us, Grey Wolf is telling me that. You are not on your own, please, please, please believe this. *You are not on your own.* Good."

Wilf left us and after a few more songs the trumpet lifted and moved towards Eric and we heard blowing through it – then "It's very hard!"

P--- was told to touch the trumpet to help the connection. It now rested heavily on his hand. We heard a whisper saying "...must do it myself." The trumpet moved across to Eric and we heard "Auntie."

Eric, "Auntie Florrie?"

The trumpet nodded (*by moving up and down*) "It's unusual."

"It is, isn't it?"

"I'm here with you." and the voice faded away.

As we sang again Grey Wolf came close "Just to say to the gentleman – I do not ordinary do this – look forward to holiday where you have not been before. Please know you have our love and you are not alone please remember this in future time. Thank you Peace and Love."

We closed this wonderful sitting.

(Eric enjoyed life for many years, only passing in 2023.)

We had many other instances of telekinesis throughout our sittings. One evening the crystal ball was gently placed between Tom's feet, the large Crinoline Lady Bell was again rung over my head (scary) – and when we put the light on at the end of the sitting we found the notepad on the floor beside the table and this message with a star from Jenny.

Saturday 4th Dec.

Our Thanks
For your love

The small bell was now on the plate mic', but no pencil. It was on the arm of P---'s chair.

That evening had also been an evening for the spirit team to experiment. We heard a voice we had named "The Presence", whom we believe was one of the scientists behind the work, suddenly speaking out of the air via the voice box.

"Good evening. If you don't mind we are going this evening to try out experiments." (*Ann.* Pleasure, please do.) "Please say what you see or what you feel. That will help us."

We began to sing all our old songs and quickly became aware of small bright lights appearing all over the room. There were shafts of light beside the cabinet and loud clicks were heard. I saw grey shapes, discs in front of me, as though people were passing, and the tabs on the bell disappeared.

After some minutes more singing, we heard his voice again "Thank you so much for your help this evening We are so pleased with our experiments. We will see the benefit of these in the near future."

Tom commented "You are speaking well tonight."

"Thank you I try to be the best that I can."

At this point another voice took over. "I take this opportunity to thank you for your time you give to us. Not only on these evenings but at other times. (*Tom.* Our hearts are with you always.) – It is wonderful. You do not realise the enormity of this. We are so privileged to have people like yourselves who will help us. (*Tom.* The privilege is ours.) ... I hope I will have the opportunity to work with you in the future. We hope you will give me your permission to work. You will not be disappointed (*Tom.* We never are!) God Bless."

We heard Grey Wolf's familiar voice say "Peace and love ... the children come to play." I asked "Shall we sing?" and a child's voice replied "Twinkle twinkle...."

We could hear the bells were gently on the move, and as we sang we heard Jenny join in. As we finished the song I said "Hello Jenny, we're pleased you enjoyed the jelly babies." and received a 'Yes' in reply before Grey wolf closed the evening with his 'Peace and Love.'

After with a short prayer of thanks when the light was turned on we found the scene described and illustrated earlier.

These are just a few highlights from our evenings together but other visitors who sat with us no doubt have special memories of their evenings in the Brayton Circle.

The circle came to an end in January 2000 when we moved to Spain. We did, however, have one last sitting with our friends on January 6th and what a night that was. We had no cabinet as that had been found a new home, and a lot of the furniture had been sold or passed on, so our lounge seemed very spacious, as was commented on by Wilf, one of our spirit visitors that night.

It seems they were very keen to get started and were taking no chances with J--- not wanting to go into trance. As she sat down, she took one deep breath and was 'away'. Moments later when Tom asked if she would open in prayer there was no reply so P--- said the prayer instead.

We started, as we always had in their own circle, singing 'Half-a-pound of tupenny rice', 'Here we go round the Mulberry Bush', during which we heard a quiet gruff "Peace and Love". J---'s guide Grey Wolf was with us already. The voice seemed to come from a different point from where J--- was sitting and having welcomed him we heard him say "Sing!"

As we sang 'She'll be coming round the Mountain' we heard him join in with his familiar "Ho-ho" in the chorus and the Crinoline lady brass bell was up and ringing. When P--- asked if it was too late to sing 'Jingle bells' the reply was 'no' as the bell was rung vigorously.

It seems we were in for a party! And what a party it was.

Just six minutes after we had started Ann felt something catch her shoulder and land behind her, as though it had been thrown. Because of the darkness we weren't to know what it was until the end of the circle.

A female voice we didn't recognise told us Grey Wolf was busy "He's up to something," and that she was the spokesperson that evening. She told us there were many there, as this was "a sad occasion but also a glad occasion because we know more than you do, because we can look a little further."

After we sang 'Catch the Sunshine' our old friend Wilf came and we had a long chat. He was speaking via the voice box in Independent Direct Voice. He told us he had moved on from welcoming 'new comers' to – once they had settled in – showing them around and "to show them what to do and tell them they can make choices... You can do stuff here that you couldn't do before. It's reet nice that ... but I'll still come here y' know." When we told him that Eric was now doing well, he replied, "I frightened him to death. I wasn't talking like that. Well, I knew he were going to be all right. It never dawned on me he take it like that."

He went on to tell us that it was more difficult to talk to us now that he had 'moved up' "It's just not as easy but it will get better. Aye, professional like."

After he left we began to sing more of the old songs, and received taps on the table and the bells joined in. I could see grey lights – shapes by the table and the sleigh bells were rung in response. When we started on 'Pack up your troubles' the trumpet started to lift and was soon moving around to greet all of us. Tom said he knew his father was there and as I started on Granny's favourite hymn 'Jesus bids us shine' the bells rang again in response and accompanied it.

While we were singing 'You are my Sunshine' there was a loud thump as the trumpet hit Tom on the head when he got the words wrong. P--- said "That was from your Mam and Dad, Tom – Sonny." Tom replied "That's right." and the trumpet 'nodded' in response. The trumpet now went across and banged J--- on her head.

Tom told 'them' "I felt that you know!" and the trumpet 'nodded' in response and drew very close to him. He thought he heard a voice through it and P--- saw a bright white light above him as he spoke.

It was time for more singing as the trumpet tapped the legs of the small table as though for the 'Can-Can'. When I suggested it there were three taps on the legs so we dah-dahed along to it with the trumpet keeping time in taps on the table legs – speeding up as it always had those years earlier.

The trumpet sank gently to the floor (as exhausted as we were I should think) but as it lifted again P--- started 'I belong to Glasgow' we joined in and found ourselves being splashed with water. Tom exclaimed "Oh, I'm soaking" and I started singing 'Raindrops keep falling....' and as Tom got the words wrong P---said "Careful Tom or you'll get a whole glass over you," and Tom was indeed well splashed again but so was P---.

Tom's answer was, "Hands wet, face wet – Great!

It was wonderful to have this amount of phenomena in our own home as a farewell.

P--- felt someone was standing between himself and J---. Tom kept encouraging them to try, the trumpet lifted again and rested on his knee. It then moved on to his hand and caressed it as though stroking him. Knowing his family was nearby Tom said "I know you're all there. Thank you very much. Oh! It's a lovely special night."

As it went quiet, I started singing 'I'm forever blowing bubbles'. This was followed by 'The Grand Old Duke of York' and during this the trumpet went near to J--- and tapped on a form standing beside her. We heard a quiet voice say "Abe" and the trumpet tapped his head. He was extremely tall, but as Tom said the sound of its 'tap' was the sound of it hitting a head not the lampshade.

P---. Hello Abe, nice to see you ... well nice to hear you.

The voice from very high up said, "All send our best love... (*Tom.* Oh lovely, thank you.) You'll feel my presence always ... Not adept at speech. (*Tom.* you're doing very well, very clear.) I aim to be a pillar of strength. Our greetings to you all."

As he finished speaking we heard two loud clicks and the feeling of love that surrounded us all was amazing. Tom was overcome with the emotion and told us he couldn't speak. With that we heard "Yes ... likes to speak," to which P--- replied "Yes he does. God Bless you friend."

There was an extremely loud click beside Tom which made him jump, and we heard Grey Wolf say "Peace and Love". As we thanked him, Tom added "You've had a good night." To which Grey Wolf answered, "Wonderful ... May you have Peace and love in your life."

Tom thanked him and we heard his final "Peace and love."

J--- slowly came out of trance having been unaware of the forty plus minutes we had sat. We then persuaded her to close in prayer and we sang our usual closing hymn 'Till we meet again', which we had used all the time in their circle as well as our own.

When I put the light on the first thing I did was to find out what had hit me at the beginning of the evening. It was an envelope. J--- immediately snatched it from my hand, saying "You're not supposed to have that till we left."

She had placed their 'New Home' card in her handbag which had been left out on the stairs, in the hall. Reluctantly, she handed it back and we found on the front of the envelope 'G W' in writing, so familiar on the spirit writings left on our pad. J--- and P--- had signed the card inside but Grey Wolf wasn't being left out of their good wishes, so he had signed the envelope afterwards and made sure it was delivered as an apport.

They had treated us to a very special 'leaving' party with all the 'tricks' in their repertoire. A wonderful night.

Thank you, Folks!

Time to Move to Pastures New

We were sad to leave our weekly sittings with Stewart and our Home Circle at Brayton, but at the end of January 2000 we 'up sticks' and went to live in Spain, about an hour's drive south of Alicante. We were made honorary members of Stewart's Circle with permission from the spirit team to sit whenever we were in the country. When I asked Freda *(spirit communicator)* whether we should sit to send our energy on a circle night she told us we would find ourselves far too busy for that.

She was right. As well as having to set up home there, and find our way around, it was not long before we were involved in helping run Edith Baker's Spiritual Centre on the edge of Torrevieja, and a monthly discussion / teaching group 30 kilometres south in the exclusive resort at La Manga.

It seemed it was to be a fallow time for our link to physical phenomena. However things were about to change. Eileen Ledger, who had lived and worked at developing the awareness of Spiritualism for many years in Spain, had found a villa and had permission to build a centre within her garden area a few miles from Edith's. While it was being finished, she held meetings in her home and there we renewed acquaintance with a medium from England whom we knew well. She too was looking to live in Spain, and we looked forward to it.

She was a good trance medium who occasionally also sat for physical – but because of her health she didn't sit very often. Once she felt able, we were asked to join her. The room we were to sit in at a friend's house was the spare bedroom and one wall was covered with mirror-fronted wardrobes and there was no way we could cover them as they were floor to ceiling. So, we arranged that the medium sat in the far corner, away from the wardrobes. Tom and the friend sat at right angles to the mirrors and I sat opposite them, alongside the medium, in charge of the light, the music and the recorder.

These mirrors were a bit of a nuisance for the spirit team, but nothing daunted, they wanted to try an experiment. They asked if we could make a luminous plaque to hang opposite the mirrored wall. I devised a luminous disc made of a light aluminium pan lid (a common item in Spain). Because it was that time of year, I was able to get a can of luminous snow spray. I painted it over with clear varnish and, while it was still wet, sprayed it all over with luminous snow pressing it down very gently so that it didn't all fall off. It was almost perfect – but so bright when charged in daylight, that for much of the circle it was covered with a tea towel. When the spirit team was ready we were told to remove the cover. I was instructed to watch the lid and the others were to look at the mirrors opposite.

I could see what looked like a blob, a tadpole shape, against the lid as the energies moved across it. The other two, watching the mirrors, could see the silhouette of a face. It seems the spirit person was standing between this disc and the mirrors. The room was only about nine feet across, so quite a small room. I didn't see anything in the centre of the room nor a face on the 'disc'. It was another way of using whatever facilities you have got. (The face wasn't identified.)

On another evening I was asked to stretch out my right hand into the darkness and I felt a small soft pouch placed in my palm, from which came five small citrine crystals, to aid in the healing of a stroke patient we were treating at home. We were given instructions on how they were to be used. He was able to move about and walk but had lost the ability to read. A few weeks later he did start to read again – and that day, as I was transferring the healing energies to him in our sanctuary, he read the title of one of the books in our bookcase. That took us all by surprise. What a breakthrough!

As we came up to Christmas the medium's child guide, a young girl, asked us to sing Christmas carols. We sang various bits and pieces from some and then we started on good 'King Wenceslas'. As we sang Tom felt something land on his toes (as usual he'd taken his shoes off). He said, "Something's hit my foot." The little guide said, "What do you get when you sing Christmas carols, Mr Tom? You get money."

And yes, when we put the light on at the close of the circle we found indeed it was a coin. But it was a very special little coin. It was a 10sen piece from Malaysia that had hit Tom. The medium said, "Look at the date."

He said, "It's 1981."

She asked, "Does that mean anything?"

1981 was the year that Tom's granddaughter had died, at the age of 10.

The family had moved to South Africa and had only been there a year when the child had an operation, and the anaesthesia went wrong.

The apported 10sen coin

That day was the anniversary of her passing.

With that particular medium the value of the coin and the date were always important. Earlier in the sitting, before all of this happened, the spirit guide had said to Tom, "Mr Tom, your little girl is with you." – meaning Susan was there with us all.

What a wonderful contact.

We were only able to sit with the medium for about a year because she found she couldn't take the heat of the summer. It affected her health too much and she returned to England.

Ray Smith and Sir Oliver Lodge

Within a couple of months of arriving in Spain we had a card from Raymond Smith who lived down at Santa Margarita, near Gibraltar. He was a wonderful trance medium who channelled Sir Oliver Lodge and several other entities; quite a team would come and speak through him, and he invited us to go and visit him.

That first September, we travelled down across Spain touching Granada, Seville, and Malaga almost into Gibraltar, to a beautiful spot overlooking "the Rock". In the mornings, June introduced us to Gibraltar – including the cheeky baboons high up on the Rock and the underground auditorium where they as a family have given a musical charity concert. In the afternoons we spent about an hour or so each day, sitting with Ray and listening to, and talking with the team. He had by then two books published[1] with teachings from the spirit team and some poems as well. It was such a privilege to listen and to speak with them, but Ray's trance had developed to such an extent that he didn't need to go into deep trance if they wanted to pass on a message to you. As they said 'you can't go into deep trance in an airport!!', but it might be important that they tell you something. So, his eyes would just glaze over and the next thing you would know was someone else was speaking to you.

One evening after Tom had given his talk on his mother's mediumship to a number of Ray and June's friends, I noticed while the others were discussing about taking photographs using infra-red cameras and all the rest of it, I saw Ray's face change, his eyelids dropped very slightly and I heard a deep voice say – "Some energy will be extremely solid and never... ever be visible." Oliver Lodge had just popped in to let me know that while they were talking about being able to take photographs of the energies under whatever

---

1. *'Nobody wants to listen and yet'* and *'For those who are willing to listen'*

conditions – 'it would not always be possible to see it, because you could still walk into a brick wall and it would be totally invisible.'

That sounds scary but it seems that is what tis possible with the energies that are available.

Some months later Ray contacted us to know if we knew of a medium who would go and give demonstrations of mediumship in a location in Gibraltar, to try to spread the message of survival – something he had been trying to do for many years. We thought our friend Angela Mac... might fit the bill and she was already booked to come and serve the centres near us the following year, we arranged that he and June should come and see her working. At the same time he agreed to give a demonstration on trance communication to our group down at La Manga.

A few weeks before they were to arrive at our home in Eagle's Nest we made a short visit to England and enjoyed a couple sittings in Stewart's Circle. The first was on one of his 'Guest Circle' nights. There were six visitors that evening as well as us. Only June and Ray of the regular circle were present so I was asked to sit next to Stewart in place of Gaynor.

The first half of the sitting was taken up by Walter renewing his acquaintance with the guests and Christopher making them happy so that they gave off the energies that was required for such an evening of phenomena. This is an essential part of the proceedings.

I then heard a deep breathy 'voice' down – about knee level – between Stewart and myself. With encouragement it grew stronger and eventually I could discern the words. There was an independent voice box through which spirit were communicating.

We encourage him to come. Tom explained to everyone it was the Independent Voice.

Ray. We can't quite hear what you're saying.

Tom. Just a bit more.

I then heard and repeated to the circle – "Believe me, it's not though any lack of effort."

Ray. Well, take whatever you need my friend.

As the voice increased we heard:

"I hope ... within a short space of time that I should be able to communicate with you all quite freely." There were many loud responses from sitters.

'Voice'. Are my words any clearer?

All. Yes.

Ray. Getting better and louder, my friend.

'Voice'. Well I can't tell you what a relief that is. Can you hear me across the room?

Yes ....(plus many other comments)

'Voice'. Well if you are not able do so I will not be able to increase the volume of my voice. (*Many replies*)

June. – It's nice and clear friend.

'Voice'. There is a great deal that I wish to say to you all but if I suppose if I were called upon to say anything of any particular import it would be this that I am speaking to you all quite independent from the medium and it had been my particular responsibility for a considerable period of time to further develop this method of communication. You must all realise that ultimately, one day, it is our intention that I should be followed by so many souls from my world and among those, I can tell you now, will be your loved ones. That is the purpose of developing this level, this method, this style of communication between us. My dear friends, I do hope that you are able to hear quite clearly ... (*Tom.* Yes – Wonderful ...)... I cannot really begin to explain to you – that to try to convey to you all this work that has taken place this evening. (*Tom..* We understand that.) To be able to speak to you in this way (*Tom.* It's wonderful.) Well, friends I feel so very privileged in one respect but I also feel so extremely ....grateful. For all that you have brought within this room this evening which has enabled me to speak with you in this manner. Indeed, for us to be able to communicate in the way that we have been able to do this evening. (*many comments from sitters*)

My friends, I hope that before we have concluded our meeting this evening we shall be able – we shall be in a position where there is sufficient energy that will enable us to be able to leave the cabinet (*many comments*). We believe we shall need a considerable amount too.

Without a break in the flow we then heard:

"I wonder Mr Harrison (*Tom*. Yes, yes sir.)... I wonder if you would very kindly do something for me, personally. (*Tom.*. Yes certainly whatev..) I wonder if you would very kindly pass my regards, my friendship and my love to Mr Ray Smith. (*Tom*. Most certainly.) ... I heard you speaking concerning him earlier this evening, and I have to tell you that I would not have missed this opportunity to convey my presence to him. You see this is the only way in which, independently, I will have for a considerable period of time to reach him. (*Tom*. Most certainly.) ...If you would just do that for me (*Ann*. We will do.) ... I would be most grateful (*Tom*. Could we ask...) Unfortunately as much as I would like to be able to do it, it is often the fact that in spite of all..... (*Tom*. Come on, keep going.) (*June*. He's gone.) (*Tom*. Come on finish what you want to say. We will be speaking to him soon.) ... Yes, please pass my regards and affection to him. Of course, you know, Mr Harrison, perfectly well who it is who is addressing you here this even.... (*Ann*. Yes, We do.) God Bless."

We all replied, "Thank you – God Bless."

After the 'voice' had left us, Walter returned and asked for the trumpets to be returned to the centre of the circle and there followed several minutes of aerobatics with Stewart out of trance and speaking to us so that sitters knew it was not him waving them about the room – a charge which has been levelled so often against mediums.

A psychic rod was then formed and several sitters were touched before it was developed into a "gripper" that picked up a drumstick and rapped rhythmically on the table.

After Walter had spoken to Stan, one of the sitters, about his development we were then asked to keep our feet tucked under our chairs as they were attempting to walk out into the circle. Shortly after this we experienced touches on our heads and hands and a voice speaking out in the centre of the room said "We know all that you do for my world. Oh my friends I do so wish to speak with you all and encourage you to continue with your work. I know all in my world desire to work in this manner to let the world know...... to work in the light and let the world know our intentions..... Bless you."

When Walter came back to close the circle Tom thanked Walter and the whole team for what they had done.

Walter replied "There is no need for thanks, Tom, as you well know. We are all co-workers together."

What an amazing evening we had had; full of phenomena for the guest sitters and for us to witness how much had been achieved in the development of the independent voice. Especially in giving us a message for our friend Ray who – despite his years of being able to pass on incredible trance teachings from a team of spirit friends – still doubted that we all survived that state which we call death.

A month later when Ray and June came to stay in Eagle's Nest we were able to play the tape to him. On hearing the voice he was convinced it was his friend Oliver and couldn't wait to have that meeting with Stewart.

While they were with us we took them to the luxurious oasis of La Manga to meet the group of ladies we met with regularly. The group were totally enthralled by Ray's demonstration of trance. Most of them had never witnessed anything like it. Besides Oliver Lodge who spoke at length we also heard from Ray's father, Harold, and Charles. The trance lasted almost 90 minutes – an amazing afternoon.

At the end of the session June played for us a recording of a part of a Gibraltar Radio broadcast on which they had asked for a song to be played for their son's birthday. They had recorded it in case he should have missed it and on playing back the tape they heard, superimposed on the song, a message for him in Oliver's voice. "Well, Mark, I'd like to add my best wishes and to say that your Stephanie ...... husband." (The music masked the ending.)

When June took the cassette from Ray's Brief case that afternoon she found that the tape wasn't at the beginning of the recording as she had expected but part way through. Baffled, she played it and we heard Oliver's voice saying – "Well now, it does indeed give me very great pleasure to be able place my voice on your magnetic tape and to hope that you have benefitted by meetings such as these."

This was a NEW addition to the tape that June and Ray had never heard before. They were as thrilled as we were. This was our first experience of EVP (Electronic Voice Phenomena) and so pertinent for that afternoon.

Three months later Ray and June made the journey to Hull to sit with the Circle. This is an extract from Ray's report of an article he wrote for publication in the psychic press.

(As this is a long report I have not changed it into the plain print.)

"....it was arranged that all would meet on the 20th August in Hull. Flights from Gibraltar to Luton were arranged and so it was that Raymond Smith and his wife drove a hired car from Luton to Hull to attend Stewart's home circle. Below is a transcript of what took place at that meeting. If there is such a thing as coincidence the names of the leader of Stewart's circle and his wife have the same names – Raymond and June.

Mr Tom Harrison opened the meeting in prayer after which soft music was played. A soft voice was heard welcoming by name all present soon after which the voice of a child called Christopher could be plainly heard making reference to the sitters and saying that there was a lot of energy present and "We shall be able to do lots tonight. Don't fall asleep Uncle Tom." Christopher said that he did not visit the circle very often because Walter was working very hard on the physical and all that Christopher did was talk.

Christopher asked to be introduced to the new visitors – ourselves – and the leader of the circle explained that we had the same names as he and his wife. After greeting my wife Christopher said that he had heard a lot of things about me but had not heard anything bad and that our visit had been planned for a long time.

Christopher also said that there were a lot of spirit people there to talk to us and that his job was to lighten the atmosphere so that the evening would be very memorable for ourselves – Raymond and June. Christopher left saying "Bye, bye."

Next came a loud voice saying "Folks, you are all able to hear my voice? I am delighted that this evening we have so many old friends. I welcome Tom and Ann back into our midst. You know, folks, you are always welcome."

After extending a welcome to all present Walter said, "I am speaking now to June and Raymond. I want to tell you something if I may. We have waited such a long time for this evening so that we can speak with you both and for reasons which will be explained later in this meeting. June ma'am, I would like you to come and sit with me. I want to talk to you. More than that I also want to do something for you."

My wife responded, "Thank you very much." after which we heard, "Okay, Okay." Walter then referred to the other Raymond as Raymondo asking if he could have the lights and asked if my wife June would change places with the other June so that my June could sit by the side of the medium. We were all asked to place our hands (palms) uppermost and to have the trumpets removed from where they were. We heard Walter saying, "June, ma'am you and I have something in common. In a moment we would like to do something which will remain in your mind for ever. My name is Walter Stinson and many years ago I worked through a medium Margery Crandon but for so many years now my name has all but been forgotten but in recent times I took the decision to return, this time to complete the task that I commenced through my 'sis' – that is to try to do what I could to prove once and for all – the continuity of life. For so long now we have worked within this circle to try to perfect the physical manifestation of my world into yours. I would like to try to give you a small example of what I mean. Listen carefully to what I say ma'am. Give me your left hand. Such a lovely hand. You have a lot of love from my world. Understand if you will that the medium is in a heightened state of sensitivity. I know that you will understand that well. Listen to my voice. Do as I ask. Place your right hand gently on top of your left. Gently now, ma'am, move your hand gently up the arm of the medium so that you can feel the strap. Gently ma'am. Move it a little higher. Can you feel the strap"?

June responded, "I can."

"Move your hand away to hold the medium's hand tightly. Feel the strap again – is it there ma'am."

My wife verified that the strap was there.

Walter continued, "Keep hold of Stewart's hand. We want to show you what we can do when we have a suitable union and folks come together in love and energy is present that we can utilise" There was then a loud crack and Walter said, "Ma'am with your right hand feel the arm of the chair. Is the strap there?" My wife responded, "It is indeed".

"You have not let go of Stewart's hand for a moment." "Not for one moment." My wife replied.

"Then you have witnessed the passing of living matter through matter." Walter asked for the light to be switched on and asked whether the strap was still on the arm of the chair. Walter explained that it was something that could be done when folks come together in harmony and love. Although June was constantly hold of the medium's hand the strap had passed through the arm of the medium yet was still around the arm of the chair. It was said that much work had been done so that both worlds could meet together on equal terms. It was explained that whenever physical phenomena took place it detracted from the ability to be able to communicate mentally as they would like to do.

Walter said that in a moment Freda would like to speak to June and asked my wife to place her hand on her knee. The strap was then given to my wife to keep as a memory of the phenomenon. Walter said that many people in our world would consider what had been done as a miracle. He then asked Raymondo for the trumpets.

The medium Stewart then returned to consciousness for a few moments asking what had taken place.

Trumpets began to move and my wife commented that the room was full of energy. One of the trumpets tapped on the floor then two trumpets began to move all around the room and even up to the ceiling. It seemed that the trumpets moved around to look at everybody there. One of the trumpets danced upon my wife's hand then moved around to touch other people. Regular sitters said that it was a spirit friend called Sunrise who was moving the trumpets. Breathing was heard through the trumpets. Bells began to ring as the trumpets continued to move to different people.

A very soft voice was heard and encouragement was given to enable the voice to become louder. "I did so want to take the opportunity to come here this evening to tell you all how pleased we are that you, have all come together in this one room – in this space. We are so indebted to you all for all that you do for our world – to bring our message of eternal life through to the people of your world. We are unable to do this alone. We depend upon you and together we make a formidable team. I hope that you can hear me." The voice seemed to come from one of the trumpets in mid-air and sounded just like the voice of Oliver Lodge.

Two trumpets then seemed to dance in perfect sequence. Walter returned and asked me if I had a question. I said that I presumed that it was ectoplasm that was controlling the trumpets and Walter confirmed this saying that we had seen nothing yet. He said that June and I had looked forward to the evening very much and said that they also had looked forward to having us there. He said that they wanted June and I to look upon the evening as an expression of thanks to us both and that they understood everything that we did. He also said that June and I were a team and that June's work for their world was invaluable. Walter said that they wished to express their gratitude to us both. June then asked Walter for a favour that the trumpet be placed on my hand but Walter said that they were going to do something better than that providing the energy continued.

I then explained that whilst I was sitting there the name of Houdini came into my mind. "Then let it go out of your mind." Walter said. It was explained that whatever took place in the past is of the past and that nothing could be changed. He said that he preferred to use the energy to be used for the present. Walter asked for the trumpets to be moved to one side so that experiments could be demonstrated to the new friends present.

The leader of the circle was then asked to arrange for my wife June to sit opposite to the medium at the table. June sat with her knees touching the table opposite the medium. Walter said, "June, I want to show you something ma'am. In a moment we will take the energy in the form of ectoplasm from the medium Stewart. Hopefully I may be able to create my own hand."

My wife explained that a large blob of ectoplasm could be seen on the table and that coming from it were four fingers. My wife said that she could feel the hand on top of her hand squeezing it and that the ectoplasmic hand felt very solid and was very brown in colour.

Freda then returned saying that she was filled with (im)patience and that although what Walter was doing was very interesting she felt that it went on and on. It was explained to my wife that she had closeness to her mother and also to her grandmother. "What is this about apples?" Freda said. My wife replied, "Apples?"

"Was your grandmother rather fond of baking dear?" asked Freda. "Did she make apple pie". "Oh yes" replied my wife." "Do you know something about a dwarf?" asked Freda. My wife explained that that she had known some dwarfs earlier in her life. The conversation continued between the spirit communicator and my wife. "Why is a Meccano set significant to you and your children?" asked Freda. My wife explained that in their earlier days she had given her children a Meccano set to help them to learn. It was explained that June's grandmother was trying to touch June and June confirmed that she could feel something. I was asked whether in my youth I had been a boy scout. I confirmed this. "Be prepared." said Freda.

June returned from the table to sit by my side. People were asked to move as far from the cabinet as possible. It was said that a further experiment was going to be tried. Raymondo, the leader of the circle was asked to play quiet music. The curtains of the cabinet were drawn back, the trumpet tapped loudly on the floor and a cool breeze seemed to come into the room as someone came out of the cabinet. Everybody could feel the presence of a spirit friend and heard the footsteps of someone walking towards us. The spirit friend stood in front of June and me and placed a hand on each of our heads. The spirit friend asked me to place my hands together. I said, "Someone has hold of my hands. It's my friend". I know it was Oliver that took my hands in his.

He then returned explaining the problems that he and his group have in trying to reach us and that all is done in love and that one day the door will be opened so that those in the earth world will have the opportunity of communicating better with those in the spirit world. He said that when that time comes, those on earth will understand better the meaning of the purpose of life. "All life is such that it is indestructible. There is only continuity. There is only love. My friends, I thank you all. We thank you all for your love for without it we would not have been able to speak with you."

I cannot explain the feelings that I had when Oliver spoke to me.

Walter then returned saying "Okay, Okay." and that what had taken place in the room that evening was a result of the love that was there.

Walter spoke to June and me saying that there would be occasions in the future when we would meet again. He said that they were working for the day when spirit friends would be able to step from the cabinet in much greater light so that all could see better.

We heard, "I want to speak to June, my daughter. It's Mum. Isn't this wonderful."

Freda then explained that tears of joy were rolling down the face of June's mother and that I looked upon June's mother as another mother. Freda explained that June and I were meant to be together and that our meeting had been planned in the spirit world. Freda said, "Nothing ever happens just by chance," and that there was always a purpose in all that transpires in our lives. We were both thanked for the mediumistic work that we do and it was said that we would continue to do it. Freda said that there were many people in both worlds who had reason to be grateful to us. It was said that people think that Oliver Lodge and I are linked together as one and that there was a third person within the partnership and that it was June, my wife.

She was told never to underestimate herself and that there were other people in the spirit world working with us.

"May the great White Spirit be with you all", were the last words that we heard from the other world.

After the meeting June explained that she had never known as much energy to be present in any meeting that she had ever attended."

* * * * *

That was the end of Ray's report but what he hadn't mentioned was what June had told me later, that the hand on her head had moved the fingers in the rhythm of the "five finger exercise". Being an excellent, diploma holding, pianist June knew this movement well. – She went on to tell us that it had also been the answer to the conundrum left behind by Oliver in seven envelopes, deposited with the S.P.R. for mediums to solve on his death in 1940 – which no one did! So what else would he have brought back to a dear friend, to whom he spoke almost daily.

A Momentous Evening

In May 2003 on our trip to England we were able to sit in Stewart's circle on a momentous evening.

Firstly, to hear an unidentified voice – known to the circle as "Vanguard" say that he was gradually being able to take the weight of the ectoplasm and hoped soon to be able to walk among us. One other sitter that evening was Katie Halliwell, now a regular sitter with the circle. Katie is extremely deaf and without being able to lip read in the darkness, over the months, the spirit team had constructed a 'psychic hearing aid'. She described it 'like wearing a helmet'. He asked if she could hear him and she replied, "I can hear you."

"Can you hear my words?"

"I can, yes."

"We have a surprise for you."

"That will be very nice, thank you."

"So perhaps for the first time I intend to retire back into the confines of the cabinet and a person will attempt to come amongst you and to greet you, Miss Halliwell. (many comments from other sitters) I shall do my best. I shall return in a short while."

Ray and the others commented on how wonderful for Katie, and June added that he had been out longer than normal.

It was another two years before the 'Voice' revealed himself as Dr Barnett, the erstwhile voice speaking through medium George Valiantine in America in the 1920s.

The sitting continued:

June heard the breathing of a person preparing to come out of the cabinet. We heard light footsteps and then a breathy female voice tried to speak. After a few seconds June could make out that she had said "It's Mum. I wanted to come to you but it is all so strange. God

Bless you." This was followed by a kiss as Katie sent her sister's love. Mum couldn't hold the form any longer and dematerialised with a light "flump", a sound so familiar to Tom from 50 years before.

She was quickly followed by another spirit. This time it was a man who spoke with a clear voice saying, "I feel so privileged and proud that I have this brief pause to come and make myself known. Miss Halliwell this is Bob here, first – the first Bob. Miss Halliwell give my regards to Bob. Tell him Bob's here – I have her – I have her – I have her. I'm so grateful to him. She ... Ena sends her love. We are so grateful."

Tom. Well done that's splendid. The energy is really tremendous tonight.

June. It must be, Tom.

Katie's friend, Ena Brake, had recently passed and here was Ena's first husband, Ron, (who described himself as "the first Bob") telling her that he 'had her' – meaning that Ena was now safely with him in the spirit world and asking her to tell 'Bob 2'.[1]

What better proof can you have than this of 'life after death'.

Ron had died when his ship went down in 1940, after just four weeks of marriage. Through spirit contact, Ron asked her to marry his friend, Bob Brake, even materialising at a Helen Duncan séance to give his blessing. Ena and Bob spent many happy years together, raising two sons.[2]

I first heard of Ron when he returned through Stewart's trance at a 'Noah's Ark' evening in Rotherham in 1995, to talk to his wife Ena. A beautiful moving reunion. It was not until I got to know Katie some years later that I knew the full story. Now here was their reunion in spirit after sixty-three years.

We then heard a very familiar voice speaking high up and away from Stewart – "Okay, Okay"

All. Hello Walter *Walter.* Folks you can hear my voice?

---

1. These recordings are available on line by choosing the audio button at: https://alexanderproject.bandcamp.com Tracks 23 & 24
2. Read their story in *"Of Love between Two Worlds"* (available at SNPP books)

June & more. We certainly can Walter .

What followed I think is so important that here is the whole transcript that I did for Katie's book *Experiences of Trance and Physical Phenomena ... Part 2.*

Walter. I have to tell you that speaking in this manner, in this way is something which is very different to the way that I normally speak. (*Tom.* Oh! Right, right.) – You can hear my words?

All. Yes. Very well. / *Ann.* Yes. It's way above my head.

Walter. I stand before you this evening.

June. It's wonderful Walter.

Walter. I will tell you that it is some time since I last worked in this manner. I wonder if I can in any way try to show myself.

Tom. If you can, we would be delighted, of course.

Ray. We certainly would Walter.

Tom. We leave it with you Walter.

Ray. You'll do your best for us and....

Tom. We'll give you all the energy you want.

Ann. There's the light! / *Tom.* There's the light!

Walter. Ann ma'am. Look upon the light.

Ann. Yes.....Watching it. Oh! there's a hand going across the front of the light ... The fingers are passing over it.

June. That's wonderful.

Walter. Of course it may appear to be such a small thing to do.

Tom. But it is a big thing.

Walter. Watch the light, Tom.

Tom. Yes I'm watching the light.

Walter. Can you see my hand?

Tom. Oh I can, passing over it, oh! tremendous!

Katie's drawing of what we saw that night.

Walter. Katie ma'am, can you see the light? (*Katie*. I can yes.) Can you see my hand?

Katie. I can, yes. / *Tom*. Passing across it.

Walter. Raymondo, see the light. Can you see my hand? (*Ray*. I can. Yes, moving over it, yes.) What a darn shame that Michael will miss out on this (*laughter*) ... June can you see the light?

June. I certainly can. It's wonderful, Walter, thank you.

Walter. Speak amongst yourselves.

June . Okay... Are you enjoying it ,Tom.

Tom. Oh no! (*joking*). (*June*. It wonderful isn't it?) It is tremendous. It's really great.

Ray. I think it shows you what they can do when the harmony's there, when the circle's right, Tom.

Ann. And the extra energy from Michael as well.

Tom. The potential in this room, it's wonderful. We don't need the trumpets flying around and those things.

June. No we don't. *Tom*. This is what we are looking for.

Walter. Ma'am can you see the light? (*Ann*. I can Walter.) Then watch, ma'am.

Ann. I can see it reflecting off the hand below it. The hand is below it and the light is shining on to it like a torch.

Ray. Yes.

Walter. Can you see my arm, ma'am?

Ann. I can. I have just realised it wasn't as wide as the hand. Yes, and the fingers there. (*Tom*. Oh, Great!) It isn't .. oh I can't say...
when you shine a light on to flesh colour..... it is slightly greeny ... but its... Yes. (*speech fades away*)

Tom. Great stuff... Real progress.

Ann. Here's the light again.

Tom. Yes here's the light again you can see it.

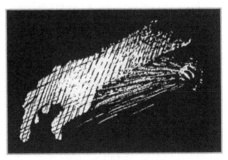

Katie's drawing of the light shining on the arm.

Walter. June ma'am, watch the light.

June. I am watching the light Walter, ...Yes.

Walter. Can you see my arm?   *June*. I certainly can.

Walter. Now is that not something, folks?   *Tom*. It certainly is.

Walter. Katie ma'am, watch the light.

Katie. Yes, I can see the light.

Walter. Tom, can you see also at the same time?

Tom. At the same time? I can.

Walter. Can you see my arm?

Katie. Oh yes I can! / *Tom*. Oh yes!

June. It's wonderful isn't it?

Walter. Now is that not something, folks?

Tom. That's something! / *Katie* That's wonderful!

Walter. I tell you this evening we have tremendous energy.

All. Good. /Wonderful.

Footsteps are heard in the room

All. There you are, there's footsteps./Good./Excellent, Walter.

Walter. Folks speak amongst yourselves.

All. Okay. We certainly will

Tom. Oh, that was tremendous. There are so many questions we want to ask. (*June*. I know.)

Tom. The first man – he walked back behind the curtain into the cabinet but I'm not sure that the second and third did. There seemed to be a thump as though they had gone.

June. On the floor. As though they had gone, yes.

Ann. Katie's Mum couldn't hold it.

June. I heard that with Katie's Mum.

Tom. Whereas Walter walked back.

Ann. Bob was so close to the cabinet, anyway.

Tom. He hadn't come out anyway.   (*Ann*. No, not very far.)

Tom. Just sufficient to speak. Tremendous!

Katie. She did extremely well. (*Tom*. Oh, Yes!)

Walter. You are most observant. (*Tom*. We try to be.) But it is important, folks. (*Tom*. Right). Can you hear my voice?

All. Very loud and clear, lovely.

Walter. I tell you, we are not always able to know with certainty whether our words are reaching you folks. (*Tom.* We understand.) – That is why we depend upon you speaking with us. Okay, Okay. Let me hear your voices. (*All reply.*)

Tom. We were right, were we, Walter, in saying that the first gentleman stepped back, you stepped back, but the others seemed to just 'thump'?

Walter. Indeed, sir, the energy, they were unable to hold.

Tom I've seen that happen. / *Ann.* They did so well anyway.

Katie. It would take a lot of practise to do this anyway. They need to practise, don't they?

Tom. Exactly. It's all a question of experience.

Walter. Ma'am, I cannot begin to explain to you the amount of work, practise as you say, that is involved in proceeding so far to develop what you are witnessing this evening. You can hear my voice. (*All.* Yes, Walter) – Yes, Okay.

Tom. It's out in the middle of the room!

Walter. I have to tell you Tom, that it is many years since I were able to retain my form in this manner – wait a moment Stewart is waking.

June. Okay Walter. / *Tom.* We leave it to you.

Walter. It is difficult for me to speak while he is as he is...... Okay Folks. I have to tell you when I speak to you about remaining perfectly still so that the energy is not disturbed, then I have to tell you, that even Stewart returning in some manner from the depth of trance that we hold him in, disturbs the vibrations and therefore makes it difficult for us to debate. (*Tom.* Right, right.)

Walter. Okay folks, I need to return.

What an evening! Four people had materialised and were able to speak to us away from the cabinet, in the space in the room. Then we had Walter showing 'himself' by means of a pure 'spirit provided' light, shining constantly on his hand for over a minute as he moved around the circle, before he 'recharged' his form with the energy within the cabinet to be able to show his arm as well.

The Circle at Los Molinos

Early in 2001 we met Robert McLernon, a Scottish medium who after visiting the area decided to come and live here as well. We eventually formed a circle with him and his wife.

Initially the four of us sat in our home, starting the evenings by using the Ouija board before moving on to trance development. One evening when they were in the midst of house hunting, Tom and I found our hands controlled by a well-known medium who had passed some years before. Having given us his initials, as he usually did, he repeatedly spelled out the price the house was on sale for. They did buy it some months later for a good deal less, but it was the right place. As well as a pleasant house and pool, there was space on the land to build a 'Lodge' for teaching and was later used for séances with visiting physical mediums. There was also a second building on the land which was eventually opened as a Spiritual centre, which they named the Acacia Centre.

Robert had sat with Stewart Alexander years some years before and he now wanted the trumpet to move in his circle, but it seems that wasn't to be his path – transfiguration and spirit teachings were more his forte. His direct voice communication was amazing. Despite Rob having a 'good' Scottish accent, many of the voices took on their own accents, although some of the teachers found it unnecessary to do so, often just deepening the tone of their voices. We had wonderful philosophies coming through from all sorts of higher levels, and I used several of them at Sunday services in various centres and also at theirs, when they opened a centre.

Spirit knows what's best for the energy the medium possesses even when they don't.

In May 2004 sitting in their home we were given an indication of what was intended for the circle. Following the child guide, Jonathan, and Sylvia who worked with the spirit children (and kept Jonathan in order), we heard a new communicator who, in a deep voice, introduced himself as 'White Eagle'. He told us he had come to prepare the way for others to speak.

I had been introduced to the teachings of 'White Eagle' when I first started on my spiritual journey back in 1991 and knew he was an evolved teacher. Was this really the same one? I sent out the thought – "If you are the teacher who communicated through Grace Cooke can you give us a sign?"

The following morning at Eileen Ledger's centre near Torrevieja, the medium, on a visit from England, was Mark Stone. When he came out of the small room at the side of the main hall he was carrying a small book, which he had chosen from the shelves there, to use for the 'reading' that morning. I could clearly see the title *The Quiet Mind*. This was a book of 'White Eagle's' teachings. Was this the sign I'd asked for?

The following week after a several minutes of communication Robert came out of trance suddenly, and we had to talk him down again. When he was settled, White Eagle came again and said "Now we have ....'the quiet mind'."

Was this a confirmation? I rather think so judging by teachings we were to receive over the following months and years.

After this week we were permitted to record the whole sessions.

In this sitting when White Eagle came he told us, "Our friends introduce themselves to you one by one. Each of us on our own vibration. Each of us communicating with each other as with you. Much organisation, much co-operation.

Tom – So we understand. Are you taking charge?

White Eagle. I am not the one (*Tom.* You are not?) – who ultimately will be the speaker and in any case our friend has his own – as you call it – 'doorkeeper' who allows us, as and when, to speak, but all of us in the team work to open the portals for he who will come to speak, who has made it known to us and it always has been known from the moment our friend incarnated on this plane. We wait. When we respect the free will, when we respect the lessons that this soul must learn, we respect that mistakes can be made; we respect the law of karma. All of these things we take into account and we wait and still we do not know the outcome. We have our aims we have our plans; we have our instructions because each of us has our job to do. (*Robert coughs and the trance is disturbed*) – I await once again the 'Quiet Mind'. (a definite confirming.)

The "friend – doorkeeper" to whom White Eagle was referring was the 'Tibetan'. He occasionally spoke to us, giving advice, or a 'splash' of his Wisdom, and as the transfiguration developed we would sometimes see his deeply lined face. Rob has a wonderful psychic portrait of him drawn by Coral Polge.

We very soon deduced that Sylvia was indeed Sylvia Barbanell the wife of Maurice Barbanell. Through Tom's friendship with him back in the 1960s, and Maurice's association with Tom's aunt, Agnes Abbott, in the 1930s, he also came and spoke to us a couple of times. We saw Sylvia many times transfigured over Rob's face, with her beautiful smile and particular movement of her head as she looked around at us all, before beginning to speak, in her gentle voice – totally unlike Rob's. She was greatly involved in helping (and rescuing) children when they passed over as they had no idea as to what had happened and were troubled because they couldn't find their mummies.

Robert McLernon

As the circle progressed, each week, as well as the regular team, different people popped in, and because we could sit with the red light, as the transfiguration developed, we had a lot of celebrities of stage and screen coming in – usually very recognisable, like Frankie (Francis) Howerd. The medium's face is quite rounded, but Frankie's face is long with heavy eyebrows – so very distinctive.

Frankie Howerd

One evening in 2005 the "faces" started to appear very quickly and we saw a big round face with a small moustache which we immediately linked to Oliver Hardy.

This was followed by Frankie Howerd again. The face changed and —here I include a transcript of the sitting:

"... the face went very narrow and the jowl drawn. He raised his hat to us and Barbara commented on his pointed nose and was trying to remember the one in the 'Carry on' films. Ann thought it might be John Le Mesurier (we had just watched a film about his life) to which a forced 'Yes' was uttered and repeated.

Ann. Good. That is why you were doffing your hat.

J. LeMesurier. Yes.

Barbara. Well done.

Ann. So lovely to have you here.

After a short pause a strong voice said 'Good evening.'

Barbara. Well done.

Ann. We can hear you clearly.

It was almost four minutes before a

John Lemesurier

long heavy face was seen with a large chin. We felt we should know the person and soon our visitor announced 'Morley'

Ann. Robert Morley?

R.Morley. Yes

Barbara. Well done!

Ann. Lovely to have you here.

R.Morley. How are you?

Barbara.. Fine thank you and yourself.

R.Morley. Very well.

Ann. You did very well indeed to show us your face.

Robert Morley

Barbara.. I knew I knew it.

The eye sockets then became very small and the lashes of the right eye disappeared completely.

The spirit person started to speak, "There are many of us who are in the acting professions or who come around.

Barbara. We are more likely to recognise you I suppose.

Spirit. Exactly so and it gives us the opportunity also of communicating and once again reaching out to those who would wish to be involved with knowing about the spirit world. It is a sad fact but a true one that those who are famous can have more influence.

Not everyone who is famous is a good person, that is not what I am saying as you will understand, but I say that those who are famous everyone knows who they are and will take note of what they are saying even if it isn't true. So what better way to get across the message of those who have gone to the spirit world ...that survive physical death... what better way than to have those who have been famous to come back and say.. 'I am still here'..

Ann. Yes. As they did so often just with a voice through Leslie Flint...but to see them would be better...

Spirit. To see and (the voice changed dramatically to a deep gravely tone) indeed hear... because now I have more control and I bring the voice also ... (*the voice changed back to Rob's lighter tone*) temporarily.

Barbara. Have we got a name?

Spirit. You understand about control?

Ann. Yes, we do

Spirit. You understand that I can, if the circumstances allow, speak very lightly through the medium's voice. I can show you my face I can speak through the medium's voice which, in effect, is better for me because I do not need to take so much control or, if I wish to take more control, I can speak through the voice of someone who has spoken (*the voice became very gravelly again*) in this way in the earth vibrations.

Barbara. We understand, that's excellent. Do we have a name? Can you give us your name?

Spirit. Suffice to say that I am a leader of men... and women...

Barbara. No, only men.

Spirit. In the time that I was leader …the time that I was leader, (*the voice deepens again*) I was known to be a leader of men.

Barbara. Oh yes.. I know

Tom. I think we've got you.

Barbara. We've got you now, thank you and welcome.

Spirit. But on a personal level I never forgot the contribution of women.

Ann. We understand that. It is great to have you here.

Barbara. It is lovely to have you here and thank you for coming.

Tom. He used to be a regular visitor to our circle at Brayton.

Spirit. I still lead. Bless you.

Barbara. Bless you my friend and thank you for coming and hope you come again.

There was a sharp intake of breath as he left and Rob opened his eyes coming partly out of trance and Barbara had to talk him back in to a deeper state

Following the close of the circle we all agreed that the first visitor was Winston Churchill – the leader of men.

Tom and I knew him from our circle in Brayton some seven years earlier when Carole and I were aware of him showing himself through Tom. We gave him then the initials of W.S.C. as an abbreviation of his name.

Three weeks later, a short time into the sitting, we saw Rob's face start to change. Tom commented, "That's a good face. Nice and steady."

Barbara. The eyes have come out now.

Ann. The nose is really broad.

Tom. Come and join us.

We then heard the gravelly voice we had heard for a few moments three weeks before.

WSC. I tried to build.   (*All.* Good, good)

126

Tom. You are doing very well. You've got the energy. You enjoy coming I know.

WSC. Good evening.

All. Good evening.

Tom. Good evening, lovely to hear your voice.

WSC. – W-S-C, I don't hang about.

All. Yes, we recognised you.

Tom. Nice to make yourself known.

W.S.C. I have much work to do still on this earth and I will work through this medium.

Tom. You do, excellent. You find him very good for you?

WSC. Even he does not know yet, but he has the power. (*Tom.* Good) ...to bring good things and I will work to bring good things.

All. Great/ Superb/ That's a great combination.

WSC. I have spoken with you before.

Tom. Not as much as you have tonight, that's excellent.

WSC. It is no coincidence that at this time I come to speak with you and to work with you.

Tom. Thank you. We want to give you all the energy to work. That is our purpose.

WSC. I take so much energy because you need to know.

Tom. That's fine, you take all you need. Lovely.

WSC. Bless you my friends.

All. Bless you/ It is our pleasure and our privilege.

WSC. You are all gathered together for a reason.

Ann. Yes we realise.

Tom. Yes we all are. Thank you. That was terrific.

And with that the face and personality were gone.

Ann. Well done, to maintain his own voice for that length of time.

Tom. And he was sitting forward like that. – Nice and steady.

As Rob started to come out of trance, Barbara said, "Steady. Just close your eyes."

Rob. Am I back now?

Barbara.. No just close your eyes.

He went back into trance and the session continued.

At the same time as Churchill made himself known there was another Star of the 'big screen' – Oliver Hardy – and later his partner Stan Laurel who made themselves known.

In April Barbara and I could clearly see a small moustache, like Oliver Hardy's, and the face was rounded too, like his.

In a sitting two months later at the start of the séance we saw the face start to move as though someone was talking and we felt we should know the face. The face fattened and we saw the small moustache. I felt it was Oliver Hardy and Barbara confirmed it and to reinforce it he started to make the finger twiggling movements so well known in the films and smiled and acknowledged our recognition. After a minute or two the face started to change and Ann initially thought it was Stan Laurel but the face continued to lengthen tremendously and we saw it was Frankie Howerd, which he acknowledged by nodding the head...... 'Yeah.'

The next week we very quickly saw the face start to change and a longer face developed and we saw raised eyebrows.

Barbara. Are you going to speak to us...... ...That's very different!

Ann. Yes, come on!

Rob shuffled on his chair and moved his hands in a distinctive manner and seemed to simper.

Barbara. Laurel and Hardy!

Stan Laurel & Oliver Hardy

Ann. I know we should. I know. We're Hopeless!

Voice. Stan.

Ann. Stan Laurel?

Barbara. I told you – Laurel and Hardy.

Stan Laurel. Stan.

Ann. Well done. I knew it wasn't Oliver.

Stan. Last week Ollie.

Ann. Ollie came last week. Stan come this week. Well done!

Barbara. That's what I said Oliver and Hardy I always get you mixed up, cos I'm only a baby. Ohh!

Ann. You have done so well. All the actions. The way he moved. Well done! ...

Two weeks later Ollie did come and we saw Ollie's face so clearly grinning and waggling his head.

Ollie. Hello.

Tom. Lovely to see you again.

Ollie.. I will speak.

Tom. Talkies now not the silent films.

Ollie. Good talking... Could do other things that would let you know who I am but don't need to.. **No, I don't need to.**

Tom. That's good, that's even better (as Ollie speaks much more strongly) really good control there, bodily control too.

Ollie. I don't need to act. **I don't need to.**

Tom. No you don't need to, just be you, with your mate.

Ollie. He's here as well.

Tom. You know you are always welcome.

Ollie. 'Cos we are just simple people.

Barbara. Well done...

We didn't get to speak with them again but were often aware of the song 'On the Trail of the Mountain Pine' (or words to do with it like 'Blue Ridge Mountains') which indicated they were around.

During this time Rob found that after a sitting there would be a large red mark on his face around his cheek, as though he had been hit. He is light skinned and doesn't tan so it was quite conspicuous. We were naturally concerned about it and so in one sitting we were told this:

Sylvia. I would also say to you. I know that White Eagle may speak with you of it if he has the chance and perhaps not, the marks that you see on the face are indeed to do with energy from – the transference of energy, rather, from the spirit to the physical. It is the way in which the physical is transforming that energy. It is similar if you like to stigmata that some people experience because of their link with the spirit world although it is not in the religious sense stigmata. It is simply that that energy is coming through into the physical and is leaving a mark in different ways. We are working with it. We are obviously aware of the distress it can cause to the medium and it is something that we would rather not have happen, but it is simply because of the reluctance, if you like, to go more deeply into the trance state at the unconscious level, and sometimes the energy is being forced through in a way that would be better if there was a greater anaesthetic.

Tom. Sure, that's good.

Ann. So perhaps once the medium understands then there will be that ease to go deeper?

Tom. But there is nothing serious?

Sylvia. No if it was more serious; I know it has been said, for we listened, obviously, to what you are saying, and it has been said that perhaps it is minor blood vessels or such like, but if it was there would be bruising in the tissues and if you notice there is never any bruising so there is no leakage of blood.

Barbara. Thank you / *Tom*. Thank you very much.

Later in the sitting, when White Eagle came we learned more:

White Eagle. It is very understandable from the point of view of the Spirit World that when there is a channel then there are so many who wait so long to speak with you and it is done in love and it is done with the best of intentions. It is my wish that many people will speak to you. Already we have come a long way.

Tom. That's true, yes.

White Eagle.. It is always better if the medium does not have a mind of their own... Sylvia has already told you of the energy transference. If it were simply a matter of stretching muscles or as she has said – bleeding – then the marks would be consistent but as you understand they are not. Even though at this stage it may not be seen there is an ectoplasmic film which we are using to mould and shape but the production of the same and the re-absorption can

130

sometimes cause a problem, as can the absorption into the physical of the type of energies needed to control and initiate such happenings, but as we work together then it is hopeful that these things will disappear.

Tom. Yes.

White Eagle. I leave you now my friends. (*All.* Thank you.)

White Eagle. Let me thank you for your efforts and dedication.

All. We thank you / It's a pleasure.

In a sitting in early March 2006 we heard from Rob's companion, The Tibetan:

"Bless you."

Tom. Bless you. Thank you for coming.

"I do not always speak to you although I am always present. I am the one known as the Tibetan ....and I am always interested in those that are on the path of discipleship. I know that in a group such as this we come together for a purpose to communicate with those in the Spirit World and to try to initiate some kind of phenomena... but very often when you meet, the initiation is taking place within you. You come together, it is not unlike the business world of your realm bringing in fact your intelligence where each brings that which they have learned and contributes to the whole. If you could see the energies that I see, that swirl and mix, the colours, the light you would find it, I believe, truly amazing.

But in giving as you do to that whole, you then ... so you learn new things. You learn from each other at this very physical level and also at a much, much deeper level, beyond the level of the soul. ... Remember at this time that those who are close to you in the Spirit World draw very near... I come to you simply to say that, while you are focusing on the result, and that is important, do not forget the joy and the illumination in the journey... I leave you now. Bless you."

I have worked with colour for many years in healing and in my auragraphs, so to see them clairvoyantly in a circle was no new thing and from the very start I found that I would see a particular colour as a spirit presence drew close. When White Eagle was drawing close I would see a deep Magenta colour and I had lately started to become aware of a strong Rose pink – a colour I'd not been aware of before and it was there that morning.

After 'The Tibetan' had left we sat for some minutes before Barbara said that it felt strange this morning and Mark, (a new sitter) agreed it felt different. I said if I had to describe it, it was like having gone up a level. Some minutes then passed before we saw big ball of light moving up and down where the cabinet was. Shortly after this we heard someone begin to speak through Rob.

"Hello."

Barbara. Welcome friend.

"At last I can make my presence known to you."

Ann. That's good, thank you.

"I have only a degree of control at this time."

Ann. You are doing well, we can hear you quite well.

"It is always better to find out who someone is from various sources but I know you all have experience, so I tell you my name when on the earth plane was Gandhi."

Ann. Oh thank you. That is our Indian connection. Thank you very much.

Barbara's stomach had been gurgling as he spoke as the energy was extracted.

Mark had a huge shudder go through the length of him and exclaimed at it.

Barbara. I have gone really cold as well. Bless you, thank you.

Gandhi. You know these signs are all confirmation ….of what is to be!

Barbara. Yes.

Gandhi. There is work to be done. All will be revealed in due course. *(All.* Thank you. Bless you.) I wish you peace.

Rob gave a strong gasp as the energy changed. A few minutes later Rob came out of trance feeling cold and with 'tears' running down his face. His head was thumping due to the rapid change in the energies that had been used.

At the end of the circle, I explained that on Sunday at Eileen's Centre, Ray Bailey, the medium that day, had said to me that he could see Indian (India) artefacts and were they going to a circle. He felt that there was a connection.

When we told Rob that Gandhi had been – he said he had seen his father's face change into that of Gandhi's with the small spectacles. We thought maybe the word father had a connection with Gandhi. We found that it did.

In a published article we found this:

"Gandhi identified himself with the Untouchables (low caste Hindus), whom he called Children of God, and introduced a system of hygiene and first aid in remote villages. Millions of followers of all classes called him Bapu, meaning Father."

Mahatma Gandhi (Bapu)

Three weeks later on March 29th, my transcribed notes record that at fourteen minutes "the colour became strong Rose pink rather than magenta and Mark (our new sitter) confirmed that he could also see it.

Barbara commented that it was a very peaceful feeling, a very happy feeling. (she shuddered) and Norman (my first husband) was there as she had just heard the name. I said that I had felt that he had been standing in front of me. We knew that they were all around.

Rob took a very deep breath and we heard "Bless you."

All. Bless you.

"Bapu here. You find me out....."

Ann. Yes we did Bapu, thank you.

Bapu. You feel the peace. I strived for peace.

Ann. Yes.

Bapu. Still I strive.

Ann. Still so much is needed.

Bapu. Today in some parts of your world the sun is blocked by the moon. The light from the sun cannot be seen.

Ann. That's right. I had forgotten that today was the eclipse. (*at the time we were sitting*).

Bapu. How can such a small sphere block out such a large light? Never under-estimate the power of the little one. When the time is right in the great scheme of things everyone can display their own power. Never think you cannot make change even when you are a little moon you can make a difference to the light of the great sun.

I see the light of each of you and know that you can do great things individually. This has been proved by mankind so many times but also I look at you collectively and I am happy because I see the soul progression that has come about because you have been able to be together. Anything else that you may experience, anything else that you may see or hear is a bonus. ... People are drawn to your circles, such as myself because of the light that is generated others may be drawn because of likes and links that you know nothing about at your physical level... I bring you peace, I leave you with peace and I wish you peace.

All. Thank you, Bless you.

We heard him withdraw as Rob took a deep breath.

The following week we had visitors from England for a teaching session and as they were well used to sitting in a dark séance we sat as usual.

After several greetings all went quiet and Tom felt the angels present. The atmosphere was very peaceful.

Bapu spoke 'Bless you friends.'

All. Bless you / T. Welcome

Bapu. Bapu.

Ann. I thought it was, welcome Bapu.

Bapu. I just wanted to say I am pleased with the work that has been done these last few days. Above all the blending of energies to bring peace.

Tom. Which was your main point. You worked for it.

Ann. I thought you'd be pleased with that.

Bapu. It was true that things had to be constructed over and over and energy put in – mental energy, emotional energy, physical energy.*

Ann. We did that didn't we.

Barbara. We did that!

Ann. And it was all of us as well.

Bapu. And that was the whole point. Everyone involved in some way.

June. I'm sure it will be much appreciated by those who come to walk that path.

Bapu. Good will come of that path. *Tom.* Thank you.

Bapu. For perhaps more people than you can imagine at this time but as always there must be progression. I speak only briefly so I will say thank you and speak to you another time.

June, one of our visitors, meditates as she walks the newly finished Labyrinth.

* Here Bapu was referring to the construction of a "Labyrinth" as a tool for meditation and prayer. As soon as I saw the space that they had in their "garden" I wanted to make a Labyrinth – having learned about them in 1993 at a Dowsing conference in York (England). This was the perfect place. Rob and Barbara and I had worked hard and long under the heat of the Spanish sun to complete it in time for our first paying students. It was well worth it and it was well used.

A month later, in May 2006, we received this teaching in one of our usual sittings:

'Bless you.'

Ann. Bless you, friend.

Bapu. Bapu.

Ann. Hello Bapu.

Bapu. I greet you my friends and as always bring you peace... I am aware of our visitors in the home.[1] ...with each new life that comes into the world it is always inspiring and encouraging because with each new generation comes new hope and new promise. It is like a gentle rain these new souls or old souls in new circumstances. They fall to the earth and bring replenishment and growth and development and sustenance but above all they bring love and hope and inspiration. ...When I was on the earth plane and saw these things happening I always thought of the legacy that could be left, the legacy that we give to our children when we pass from this world of the earth to another. What would we leave behind... and all that we leave behind is valuable. ... In some cases it is wisdom or a sense of justice; in some cases it is material wealth or possessions which can in their own way be very, very important because if basic needs are taken care of then a more spiritual energy can be allowed to manifest.

For too many people on the earth plane that is simply the case that they are too busy trying to stay alive and one day perhaps then the legacy that will be left will be education, that there is enough for all. Change is inevitable, change is necessary because we are dynamic beings whether in the spirit world or in the physical world, so we are constantly changing and evolving. It is the direction that we go in that is so important and we learn from those who go before us, so always we have a responsibility to those who have gone before us and to those who come after. ... I will leave you now friends for I know that other people may wish to speak, and I was never one for hogging the limelight."

Tom. No, we know. Thank you.

Bapu. Bless you friends and thank you.

Ann. Bless you.

---

1. Rob's son, Bobby was visiting with his wife and baby daughter.

However, five months later, on October 26th, there came a particular request from Bapu.

"Bapu"

Ann. Hello Bapu, thank you.

Bapu. We use your energy.

Ann. It is good to hear you again.

Bapu. It has been some time but we make you a channel for our peace.

Ann. Thank you. (*My address in the service on the Sunday had been on Peace.*)

Bapu. And those in the Spirit World who wish to make changes unite with us. … Yes, your room is very busy. Many people come and join us. … If you would have the name Dhaka in your mind.

Ann. We will.

Bapu left us and we sat for 2 minutes, directing peace and healing. There was a huge double crack like gunshots behind Tom in the bookcase. Leonie became very cold and Ann was very hot.

A further three minutes passed before we heard Bapu say, "Thank you for your efforts."

Tom. Thank you Bless you.

Bapu. Bless you.

A couple of minutes passed before Rob announced he was back with John Lennon singing 'Imagine' in his head. Rob took a while to be able to move and then we did the healing.

As Rob closed the circle, he told us he had Amun-Ra in his head, the Sun God.

Rob had also been aware of the Nazarene being around, and Raphael in the background and they seemed to be orchestrating things. Rob saw the subcontinent of India. He could still see people around as we were talking.

TWO days later there was a political uprising in Bangladesh particularly around Dhaka. The following is a report from the internet at the time:

"12 killed in Bangladesh clashes"

Violent protests have continued in the Bangladeshi capital of Dhaka as the man due to takeover as interim leader ahead of elections withdrew.

"More than 15,000 policemen have been deployed in Dhaka

An official of Bangladesh's ruling party was hacked to death on Saturday as the death toll across the country rose to 12, and 2,000 injured, police said on Saturday.

The Bangladesh Nationalist Party (BNP) official was attacked by supporters of the Awami League, the main opposition in the southern region of Bagerhat, Bahadur Sharif, a police officer said. "He was hacked repeatedly with machetes and died on the spot," Sharif said.

Seven others were killed on Saturday as thousands of supporters of the opposition parties and the ruling BNP went on the rampage, clashing with police in the capital and elsewhere.

Police clashed with nearly 10,000 demonstrators who tried to hold a banned rally in the city centre. Around 100 police officers were also injured, police said.

Riot police fired tear gas, rubber bullets and warning shots into the air to disperse thousands of protesters who were throwing stones."

I hope that our energy helped to reduce the violence which the spirit team had seen coming.

* * *

Many came, we were told, just to practise their skill in showing their faces in order to be able to work with other mediums who were developing and to make themselves known easily, to show how genuine this transfiguration phenomena was – not just 'Dad' coming when only one person could recognise them, but a lot of people would recognise them. Buddy Holly, John Denver, Brian Jones, Ray Mullard, Max Wall, Lord Dowding were just some who 'dropped in'.

One of my favourites was Liberace and we would occasionally see many sparkling lights in the room before we saw his smooth face and heard him (as well as occasionally seeing his sequined tuxedo sparkling in the red light). Sometimes Barbara and I would clairvoyantly see the candelabra as well. He was lovely to chat with. We often listened to his music on a CD at home and in the car, and I would tell him when we'd been listening to his music and he'd reply, "I know you have." in a particularly knowing way and his lilting American accent. (No sign of the Scottish accent of the medium.)

In March 2007 he spoke for much longer than he had done before. There were just the four of us sitting that morning and ten minutes in we heard an American voice sing 'I hear music' – the sign that Liberace had come.

Barbara. Welcome / *Tom.* Good!

Liberace. 'And there's someone there'.

Tom. That's right. How are you this morning?

'You've gotta have glitter'

Liberace. I'm very well. I have George with me also. I am very much learning how to do this and George helps me.

Tom. That's good. Well done. (A. Great.) Well, when you've learned more we'll have to have the music (the keyboard) in here and you can play us a tune.

Liberace. I would love to do that.

Ann. That would be wonderful.

Liberace. It brings such joy and light into peoples' lives.

Tom. It certainly does. You're right. Excellent.

Liberace. Entertainers are much needed. In whatever form they come.

Tom. Our friend in England, a lady who had a stroke, loves your music, plays it a lot, so I'm sure that helps to heal her, as well.

Liberace. The power of music to heal is as yet relatively untapped. People feel it and of course there are some enlightened souls who use music as a therapy but I think in time to come, when people are more aware that the power of music will be recognised even more than it is now. (*Tom.* Good.) Right now people use it for entertainment, or when they are sad, when they're happy. They use it to go and meet people. It is such an important aspect of society, (*Tom.* It is.) – but when you break it down and all the different kinds of music come to light, then it is the rhythm, the vibration behind the music and wherever people are in the world they respond to the rhythm even the most, in inverted commas, primitive of civilisations need rhythm. They use basic rhythm and vibration, and it is like all other things of this nature there are different levels and it becomes more elaborate. As it becomes more elaborate the message becomes more subtle but nevertheless it is the same message.

Ann. Like some of the chants that have this hidden sound within them.

Liberace. Indeed and all over the world again from the most primitive to the most enlightened, if I can put it that way, chanting using the voice is so important. It is the expression of the rhythm that people feel, whether it is Gregorian chant or Buddhist chants, it doesn't matter the repetition of the rhythm and vibration is so important.

Tom. Were you aware of the value of music in healing when you were here?

Liberace. Not in the way that I am now. If you can imagine that I was aware of the effect it could have on people or even aware, if you like, of the effect that I could have on people which is not necessarily intended in the first place but I allowed myself to develop into someone who could have a persona which people could respond to that is not necessarily the whole me. There were other parts of me that didn't particularly like what I was doing if you can understand what I'm saying, (*Tom.* Yes.) ... but it was... I followed the path that was laid out for me, if you like, and I find that by being that person then I could bring a whole heap of love and light and joy into the world. People liked it and of course I ... that was secondary to the fact that I enjoyed the music that I was playing and composing and sometimes that's true we have to become someone that we are not and we have to allow that part of us to shine so that we can do the job that we have come to do. I know that in the mind of this medium, the bloke that I work with and have been around, as I am around all of you, that there are many thoughts concerning who is successful in the world and what makes success in the world and how you measure success in the world. It seems sometimes that those who are the most arrogant, the most selfish, the most uncaring are the people who are the most successful. (*Tom.* Often.) It depends on what they have to do but they are tapping into something in themselves, which is basically self-belief and when you believe, because we are always told this, when you believe – you can make anything happen. (*Tom.* Hmm, Yes.) and we always think about that being out in the world somewhere, that if you want it to happen then you can make it happen but basically you have to believe in you and it has to be a true belief. If you do that then you can achieve anything, because nothing will stop you and you are able to put aside sensitivities, you are able to put aside the caring side of yourself because you have a goal and you want to get there and you do it. That can be a good thing or a bad thing, but it is a true thing. (*Ann.* Yes.) ... Well I've taken up enough time (*Tom.* Lovely to have you.) ... I will speak with you again.

Ann. Lovely to talk to you / *Tom.* Please.

Liberace Keep smiling.　　　(He had spoken for 8½ minutes)

This certainly made us think.

Shortly after that we were told by George (Rob's main spirit 'companion') that Liberace preferred to be known by the name "Archie", and we were happy to do so. We felt he was now a close friend – well at least Tom and I did.

Some time later we were advised by a friend, Hylton Thompson, who had specialised in séance room lighting, to bounce the red light off the back wall of the new small séance room (a very light colour) to make it more diffuse. By doing this shadows / highlights on the face were reduced and faces were more discernible. Now some well-known political figures, were very clear and recognisable in the red light. Although they didn't speak, when we voiced who they were we would either get a salute, a 'thumbs up' or some other acknowledgement of recognition. They always made their presence known at one particular piece of music in our selection.

In 2009 we had one very special spirit visitor, who was instantly recognised by Tom and myself, and that was Ray Smith from Gibraltar. We knew him well, having stayed with them several times and helped when Mary Duffy was at his home giving sittings. When, using this new lighting, I saw the face I felt it might be Ray.

For once Tom was not relaxing – with his eyes shut – giving all his power for whatever might happen, but giving encouragement to whoever was trying to show himself. Tom then realised that he knew who it was. A voice huskily said 'Hello.'

I encouraged him, "Come on then."

Tom. Yes you can ... that's it ...(*as the face strengthened*)

Voice. Ray ...Ray!

Ann. Yes, it's Ray, I thought it might be. Listen to the tone ... Fantastic. It's good to see you.

Tom. Have you met any of your friends?

Ray. All of them... Oliv....

Ann. (*laughs*) So now you know.

Ray. It's not how I thought it'd be.

Tom. Splendid / A. Well done.

Tom. Do you want us to tell June?

Ray.. Yes ... Yes Please! ... Glad you can hear me?

Ann. So are we.

Tom. That's quite quick!

Ray. Yes

Ann. You had many years practise. Brilliant, Well done.

Ray. Bye

Ann & Tom. Bye. Talk to you again.

The sitting was as usual being recorded and when we sent that portion of the recording to the family, just the way he had said 'Yes please' convinced his wife and others around Gibraltar that it really was him that had come back. In fact, one of the people who heard the tape was so convinced it was him they wrote to *Psychic News* saying 'Ray Smith has returned'.

He was a very special visitor – to know that a friend had been able to drop in just nine days after his passing and to be able to confirm his survival to the family, was a wonderful gift for us all.

142

In August 2022 when I told the audience of this at the International Spiritualist Federation gathering at Cober Hill Hotel in Yorkshire, one of the delegates, Agnes, confirmed that she had heard the recording, and having known Ray many years before, had recognised the voice on the recording.

Although having been a trance medium Ray for many years was still not sure that he would survive death until, as he wrote in a letter to Tom, after he had heard Tom give his talk and read his book a second time.

Raymond Smith
New Year, 2006

"Dear Tom and Ann,

Tom – having read through your book the second time I feel impelled to mail you. I must confess that when I read it the first time I did not take enough time reading everything and therefore, missed some important bits. Even though I enter that trance state I have always thought that it could be my sub-conscious mind having read some of Oliver's books and been doing hypnosis since I was about eighteen. Anyway, I am trying to say that your experiences recounted in your book have helped to turn belief into knowledge that there really is another world that Spiritualists call the spirit world and to accept that it really was Oliver that managed to come through Stewart when we were there. Also in reading your book it made me realise your present age. I thought I was getting on a bit – 79 next birthday but it seems you can surpass me by a good ten years. I have had to accept the fact that physical phenomena is more convincing than mental, except in one or two exceptional cases. To make this mail short let me once again say that your book is a treasure and I feel that all Spiritualists should read it. It would be lovely if we could sometime meet again before going home but as you know June's health is not too good these days. Still let us hope and pray that we do meet again – on earth I mean, the consolation being that we certainly will in the next.

Your good friends June and Ray"

We received that letter on 7th February and on July 13th he joined his friends in the spirit world, but he was back with us on the 22nd – only nine days after his passing.

I have already mentioned Sylvia Barbanell and Tom's friendship with her husband, who was the founder of Psychic News in 1932. Because of this link with Tom, he came to the circle in September 2005.

We shortly saw Rob's face crumple and become very lined as he held his chin in against his throat. This face faded and we saw a smooth rotund face. Ann saw tiny sparkles of light between Tom and Rob. Again the face changed and the head turned.

Barbara. Hello friend. ... It's Sylvia. Hello Sylvia.

Sylvia. Hello.......How nice to be with you at this level again.

Ann. Good to hear you.

We could see that she was listening to someone in the Spirit world. After a minute or so we could see the face change to a deeply lined face and someone was making a great effort to speak.

Ann. Come on friend, you are doing well.

Sylvia Barbanell

Then we heard the Voice say what seemed to be Wallace.

Ann. Hello

Voice. Hello...Hello. Hello.

Ann. Hello. You have done well.

Voice. ...Made the link through Sylvia.

Realising it was Maurice Barbanell who was speaking Ann said "Good. ...Tom are you watching?"

Maurice. Hello. (*speaking towards Tom*)

Ann. Darling, it's Maurice.   *Tom.* Who?

Ann. 'Barbie'

Maurice. 'Barbie'

Tom. Hello Barbie.

M. Barbanell. Hello.

Tom. Lovely to see you.

M. Barbanell. And you.

Tom. Thank you for coming. Great.

Ann. Great, watch the face.

Tom. Are you still busy?

Ann. Yes, you can see it. Watch the face, Tom.

As we watched we could see the face had spectacles on.

Tom. Yes, I am… He had glasses on!

Ann. Yes, he did.

Tom. Hmmmm……Well done.

Maurice Barbanell

M. Barbanell. I have the dice ... I like to take a chance… was never afraid to take a chance. No, no. You know… Exciting!

Tom and 'Barbie' chatted together for a couple of minutes about *Psychic News* and old times and then we heard him say:

M. Barbanell. I did what I had to do.

Tom. And you did it very, very well ... as you know, you and Swaff together.

M. Barbanell. And of course we are all still linked… the work goes on.

Tom. That's good. Yes Splendid!

M. Barbanell. I have to go now.

Tom. Thank you for coming. Try again some other time.

M. Barbanell. Bless you friends, I will try again.

Tom. Bless you 'Barbie' and Sylvia.

After a few moments we saw Sylvia again.

Ann. That was lovely, thank you

Sylvia. Yes…. It was my intention to pass a message on but I thought it would be better coming from him and fortunately circumstances allowed me to do so.

Tom. Good, the energy was there.

Sylvia. And of course we work as a team so it is necessary to be allowed to use some of the energy available, because it is sometimes required for something else.

Tom. Yes understood, that was really good.

Sylvia. I'm sure he will be back.

We didn't hear from him again but six weeks later we had this unexpected visit.

... After two minutes Barbara turned the light on, and Tom said he had just thought that Silver Birch was with us today.

I saw a strip of bright light on the wall beside Barbara about four inches long. This was seen twice.

Then someone spoke through Robert – "Bless you."

All. Bless you friend

Voice. I am privileged to be allowed to speak with you.

Tom. Lovely. Thank you.

Voice. Yes, when my instrument and friend was on the earth plane, I was indeed the one known as Silver Birch.

Ann. Thank you. / *Tom.* Thank you.

(*Rob gasped as he took a deep intake of breath.*)

Barbara. Gently. Steady, steady (*as Rob's body jerked again with another intake of breath.*)

Tom. No wonder I sensed him so strong. Steady. Thank you very much.

Silver Birch. We are always interested in what is happening within our group soul.

(*Several noisy deep breaths were taken.*)

Tom. You find the conditions here very good?

Silver Birch. Yes, I take some time to play the new instrument.

Tom. Yes understood. That's good.

Silver Birch. And as you are well aware there are many who will speak. There is wisdom from our side to be transmitted – but all in good time.

Tom. We understand.

Ann. Did you mean, Silver Birch, that by 'the group soul' that we are part of that same group soul?

Silver Birch. Yes indeed.

Ann. Thank you. It is a great privilege.

(There was a deep shuddering gasp from Rob)

Tom. Wonderful. Oh God, yes! (*shuddering, as we felt the immense loving energy amongst us*)

Silver Birch. We move among you.

Ann & Tom. Yes, yes, we felt you.

Silver Birch. Yes and I feel from where I stand and look, despite misgivings on the part of the medium at times yes good things will come.

Tom. Good things are happening now.

Silver Birch. Yes. I am able to draw close in a way that I have not done for some time, although I work with many people, you understand, but... for us too it is sometimes welcome to remember how it was.

Tom. Oh right, with your previous medium.

Silver Birch. And with whom I still work in the Spirit World.

Tom. Like Sunrise still works with my mother.

Silver Birch. Indeed. We pledge ourselves, sometimes for a long time if you can understand time in your sense. It is not the same in the spirit world, but we pledge ourselves to do a particular type of work whether that soul is incarnated in the physical or not. (*Tom.* Right, right).... Because the work goes on (*Tom.* Yes, that's right. Lovely.)... It is through the contact with my friend and also with the lady that I am able to speak so quickly.

Tom. Yes. Through Sylvia and Maurice.

Another noisy intake of breath was followed by "Peace be with you."

Tom. Thank you for coming / *Ann.* Bless you.

There was a long noisy out breath and he was gone and was immediately followed by Sylvia.

Tom & Barbara. Hello Sylvia.

Ann. That was wonderful.

Sylvia. For us too. Yes, indeed wonderful. We are indeed privileged.

Tom. Thank you for opening the door.

Ann. A wonderful soul.

Sylvia. Barbie never could keep his nose out of things could he?

Tom. Ah, but it was for the best.

Sylvia. But we are indeed privileged that these great souls come to speak with us and are interested in what we do.

Tom. We are privileged, greatly privileged.

Ann. It brings a great responsibility too.

Sylvia. I will speak with you again.

All. Thank you.

Two months later he came again. That morning we had had a new sitter join the group and it was after White Eagle had spoken for a short time that Rob took another deep breath, and we could hear someone drawing close. A very gentle voice then spoke to us:

"Bless you friends. Once again I am privileged to speak with you.

Ann. It is our privilege, an honour.

"I am the one known as Silver Birch."

Ann. Thank you, friend.

Silver Birch. As I have said before, I learn to play a new instrument.......... And I too welcome Leonie and Mark to our circle. I have not spoken with you before… although I understand you have seen a not very good likeness of me.

Ann. That's right.

Silver Birch. I am really much more handsome. As you know it is how we represent ourselves through the mediums and is not necessarily how we are seen by our spirit friends......

I speak with you only briefly, because with the new energies that are present much work is being done behind the scenes… But I will speak with you again and I hope that you feel the joy that I bring you and the love that I feel for those that do this work, accessing the spirit world. Bless you friends.

All. Bless you.

Tom. Thank you for coming.

Here he was telling us that because a new sitter had joined us they were having to absorb and adjust the energies that they had to work with.

It was another year before we heard him again and this time he gave us philosophy.

... We quickly heard a deep intake of breath which sounded like White Eagle but it was another couple of minutes before he spoke. The wind was very wild outside but the room was extremely peaceful. Barbara felt breezes around her and no sooner had Ann said the magenta was very strong than White Eagle spoke:

"Bless you. White Eagle speaks with his friends".

Ann. Thank you, White Eagle.

White Eagle. And I can tell you that today we are blessed with the presence of our other friend, the one known as Silver Birch. I know it is some time since he has spoken with you but nevertheless he is on many occasions around us.

Tom. Good, good.

Three more minutes passed in quiet, before Barbara said she could sense green but not see it, while Ann had been aware of all of us being in a high place looking down over green fields – very peaceful. Another two minutes passed and Rob started to speak in very much his own voice, but deeper. We took this to be Silver Birch from the content of what he said.

"Many words have been written in your world and transcribed from those in our world on the meaning of life. They are great works of philosophy, on the levels of being and on enlightenment ... and yet still there is never a complete understanding.

What we learn... is to trust the perfection of the Divine Plan. We learn to accept whatever is, at any given moment ... and to use our wisdom and awareness on the course of action to be taken next.

The whole process is one of refinement... and because much of that refinement is coming from a level above that which we fully understand, then we never can fully understand why things happen to us; why we feel the need to create other things in our life.

It is all of Karma and we create Karma. We are dynamic beings and therefore can never be totally still.

But we can try to still our minds as much as possible and find that peace within and the bliss that comes from knowing... that there is a link to the Divine... and that whatever happens we will survive... and that we will go on to better things, ... to evermore enlightenment.

I wish for you that peace."

A year later, in November 2008, I read this to the assembled congregation at the dedication of the Acacia Centre. A good friend who was present recognised it as Silver Birch's phraseology.

These are some of the highlights from seven years of sittings in this circle. After Tom's passing the circle changed and with new sitters we had more similar experiences. I will close, however, with one of White Eagle's teachings from 2005 and the feelings we had of spirit presence later in that séance.

White Eagle. Yes, I have a very powerful energy... I jest. ... I hear the medium today talk of lines of energy that join us together... as we go from incarnation to incarnation in the physical world there a certain points in that particular lifetime depending on the aim of the soul and the personality then we pick up, quite literally, the threads of that which we are, so the links that exist between us and the spirit world perhaps if you can imagine then we pick up again when we incarnate in the physical world... but always we have free will.

But there will be an inner drive an inner energy that wants us to pick up those threads and develop that which we have spent time developing before... and it never ends... It is very true that the more we know the more we know how little we know... (*Mark.* How true.) But there is much joy to be had in knowing that no matter what life throws at us in the physical world that it will go towards our own soul growth no matter what choices we make we learn from them. (*Tom.* We do, yes) ... It is just as valuable to experience unhappiness, pain and suffering as it is to experience joy and love... and nowhere else can you experience such a diversity of emotion as on the physical plane.

Tom. So that is the purpose of coming back ... coming here, is it?

White Eagle. Indeed, that is why so many souls wish to experience that which can only be experienced in the physical world. (*Tom.* Right.) When I talk of the physical world I talk not only of the physical Earth because there are other worlds that are physical. (*Ann.* Yes.) ... but the earth plane itself... the Earth planet itself has its own peculiarities with regard to choice and therefore is attractive to those who wish to learn to make right choices. (*Tom.* Right.)

I leave you now, my friends while those who wish to do other things within the circle are allowed to do so.

All. Thank you. Bless you, White Eagle.

Much later in the sitting we heard White Eagle say, "Now we walk among you."

Ann. Good.

White Eagle. I tell you we are happy with the vibrations which we have. We work to make the trance deeper. (*Ann.* Good) ... Then we can release more of that energy that is required to do the things that we want to do. As you know every séance is an experiment ... and it is fun for us to do also.

Ann. Good. Because you never know what to expect I suppose with the energy that is here.

White Eagle. We never know exactly how it will turn out although we have obviously a plan and expectations and we can usually predict, because of our experiences but never-the-less nothing is ever guaranteed. There are many variables between your world and ours; how each individual is on the day; what has been happening in the mind; what has been happening with the physical. But each time we meet we say this is what we have today. You may now feel the change in temperature.

Ann. Yes, my right leg has gone absolutely freezing.

Mark. Yes it is colder.

White Eagle. It is because of those in the spirit world coming closer because the vibrations allow us to be more physical and although I am not there to feel it the same as you, I know the feeling that you are likely to have.

Ann. There is a very distinct tightening at the back of my head.

Barbara. I just had a couple of shivers. Ooo, there is another one.

Ann. They are getting very close to you.

Mark. I seem to get quite a lot of emotion with White Eagle when he comes through.

White Eagle. It is at this time you may see the orbs or lights.

Barbara. There are loads of white lights around. Just like it is all lit up with white lights.

Ann. There is a cool breeze down the right side of my face too.

Mark. Oh dear. (*and he shuddered*)

Barbara. A shiver right from the top to the bottom. There is someone definitely with us, Mark.

Mark. Really is. Oo dear. (*shivering*) It doesn't stop.

Barbara. Still a lot of white lights, isn't there?

A couple of minutes passed in quiet before we started to warm up but Barbara had another shiver and we heard the familiar gravely voice of W.S.C. say "I am still here." (*Ann.* Good.) "They were just giving you a hug."

Rob's breathing became much more throaty, and we thought someone was going to speak and another minute passed before Barbara and Mark both yawned and Barbara became really cold again. Three more minutes passed before Jonathan, Rob's "child" guide spoke to us.

Jonathan (Rob's 'child' guide). Hello.

Barbara. I thought you weren't going to speak this week.

Jonathan. People were busy. I had to let them in quickly… Mr Churchill was here.

* * * * *

The experiences in this circle were not confined to "physical" phenomena such as trance speaking – with communications from spirit companions and evolved teachers, and transfiguration effects by well-known people, celebrities and musicians. We had also experienced changes in temperature, emotion and frequently saw various colours when certain spirit people were drawing near. We had joined in healing sessions and had sent peace to where it was needed.

This was a time of growth and learning on a different level, and it was a privilege to be part of it.

The Acacia Centre opening ceremony with Mrs Edith Baker of the Baker Foundation in Torrevieja, Barbara and Rob McLernon. November 16th 2008

Spirit Teachings at the Acacia Centre

Home Circle, March 18th 2009

White Eagle and The Tibetan:

"Bless you friends. White Eagle speaks with his friends. Once again it is a joy to speak with you. We look forward to our meetings when we can express ourselves. We know it is not possible every time, but every time you sit and contemplate or meditate then we can draw close to you.

If you can imagine for us in our world where we see a plan we can have a strategy for working out the game it is like a chess board a giant chess board where we try put the pieces in the right place at the right time but we have our strategy worked out if you will, and we know when things should happen and where they should happen and with whom they should happen. Our job is made more difficult because with our chess board the pieces can run off, they do not stay where we ask them to stay but it makes it more interesting and more challenging if you will.

And with you sitting in groups or by yourself you are making yourself more aware and so when you are asked to do a certain thing then you know that we are influencing you and you can respond accordingly and then everyone is happier …if we can ever be truly happy."

After only a moment's break we heard the different voice of the The Tibetan:

"Bless you friends, I talk to you today about order and ritual – the qualities of the Seventh Ray that is manifesting more and more in your world. It can appear that many things are fragmenting as the old order slips away – the order of power from a central source perhaps because the new order is more about smaller groups that are linked together while still maintaining the order that is needed; the knowledge allied with wisdom can emanate from each group and be lighted to other groups around your world. It is beginning now, it has been going on for some time but I tell you this because it is important for your small circles and your larger centres the moment they are linked, you can see the link that takes place through your computers and the internet. I can assure you it is only the beginning and you will feel that manifestation ever stronger, so therefore, every time you sit in your small groups even if there are only two or whether there are forty-two it doesn't matter, the energy is used to link to the network and allied to those groups and the order they produce. The ritual is also important, the seventh ray is also the ray, I know has been said, of Ceremonial Magic but you must think of it in a different way from that which you have thought before. The Ritual in any kind of Magic is only a means of focus, it is a means of strengthening that which is in the mind but the new order is very much a Mind order.

The Network of your Internet is only a physical manifestation if you like, of the link up through the mind. If you had an awareness that was possible to link even stronger in the mind then you would not need the Internet because you would just think and be able to direct those thoughts to one or to many, and they would pick it up telepathically, and they would understand from whence that message came and to how many other people it had been given.

I cannot emphasise enough the importance of the focus of the mind. In your meditations and contemplations if you need to go over the same thing time and time again then it is no bad thing it will make those thoughts real. And the more you do it the more powerful it becomes."

Tom asked, "Is there any specific purpose we have to concentrate on?"

"At this moment in time simply concentrate on sending those thoughts into the ether, and trust that those who direct energies will use them in an appropriate way. Of course within this there is also the need to be open-minded about the communication from the Spirit World and the other worlds, because it is that communication and that co-operation that will enable Man to adapt to the changes in the

Earth. Much is said I know about the damage that mankind can do to the Earth but I would suggest to you that it is also about being in tune with what is happening with the changes that take place so that mankind itself can adapt and learn to live with those changes.

Far too often there is information from the Spirit World about the changes which need to be made by mankind, for mankind needs to be rooted in one place. We talk about the chess board earlier and how people can run off the chess board, but sometimes people do not want to run off the chess board nor do they want to change position also. So they stay oblivious of the energy they are creating by staying – oblivious of the resistance they are causing by their inflexibility.

The Earth, as you know, is a living, changing, growing being and therefore there will be change because the outer always reflects the inner. So if there are changes, there are changes within the Earth's Inner Being and there will be changes in the outer manifestation of that being. And Man must learn to adapt, change and adjust –and that starts with each individual, then with your small groups, then with your centres.

Change will come and all be positive.

Bless you friends."

* * * * *

Home Circle, August 12th 2009

Overshadowing and Reflection

White Eagle and Silver Moon:

"Bless you friends. White Eagle speaks with his friends. It is good to see you all here once again. I hear you speak of overshadowing. From my standpoint it would be fair to say, as a medium you are always overshadowed by someone. The Great Spirit overshadows all but it is the degree to which you are aware of the energy that surrounds you that determines how much you feel overshadowed or indeed see someone else being overshadowed. All that you transmit in the medium's state is a reflection of that which comes to you from the higher level and the more polished your mirror is then the truer the reflection. If the mirror is dirty or dusty and has lost its sheen then it cannot reflect correctly that which is thrown into it. Information goes into the mirror but it does not reflect it truthfully so that others can see the purity of it."

Silver Moon continued this theme, in a deeper – stronger voice:

"And all is a reflection. In many ways the development of the disciple upon the path is akin to the scientists who love to disintegrate all that is in front of them and analyse each thing individually. The disciple upon the path must differentiate between the energies that they see, hear or feel so they are aware of the different aspects of the Universe, and in so doing eventually that disciple will reach the conclusion within themselves, a knowledge and an understanding, not a belief, that all is indeed one and that all is a reflection of the other.

There are those who look to the stars, some to the Universe and to black holes and other modern expressions they use to explain that which has been for ever – with each discovery they give it a new name but it has always been.

There are those who go smaller and smaller into the atoms and the nucleus, discovering particles of energy or mass and both, and give new names to that which they find, which has always been. And those who look smaller and those who look larger eventually will come to the same conclusion – they are the same.

One is a reflection of the other. As above so below... I hope I am not boring you... When we look outside ourselves we must to some extent unravel the energies that drive us and guide us and then when we understand them we realise that we are whole and that we are part of a greater whole and that greater whole is part of an even greater whole. We are a reflection of the light from the Divine Spirit and therefore we must endeavour to polish our mirrors.

Bless you."

* * * * *

International Physical Mediums at the Acacia Centre

Following Tom's passing in October 2010 I had many contacts with him through trance mediums, as well as through mental mediums, and these are all recorded in detail in my book *Harrison Connections*.

At the Acacia Centre the following August they held their first 'Festival of Physical Mediumship' with David Thompson. David travelled with Christine Morgan from Australia to give us a week of teachings, demonstrations and three séances.

This is the report I put out on my website:

"This week the Acacia Centre in the Murcia region of Spain held its first International Festival of Physical Mediumship and what a great week it has been – full of laughter, friendliness and phenomena – as well as fascinating 'educational' sessions on trance, physical and mental mediumship.

People came from across the world, some staying all week, others just two days – Circle members came in support, from Australia and England; and there were participants from Brazil, Portugal, Florida and Los Angeles; from Norway and Sweden, Denmark, Switzerland, UK and all over Spain – a truly International gathering, and with one purpose to touch the Spirit and join the two worlds together. Some were experienced but most were first time sitters.

The week started on Sunday afternoon with David and Christine talking about trance and his development. This was followed in the evening session by David being entranced and his guide William answering questions from the audience – some very good answers too.

I noticed particularly when David speaks naturally he has the Londoners' 'f' instead of 'th' – like Billy Cotton's 'forty fousand feathers on a frush' – for those old enough to remember it. When William spoke this aberration was absent.

He explained to us that ectoplasm was used to coat David's vocal cords so that he could speak in his own voice but because the ectoplasm was still within the body, the light of the room was not affecting its production. A most enjoyable evening with lots of humour.

Monday afternoon saw two speakers relating occurrences in two very different circles. I spoke about 'The Mediumship of Minnie Harrison' and Robin Foy on his 'Scole Circle' – a good foundation and probably 'mind-boggling' for many who were attending a physical mediumship event for the first time and had never sat in a physical circle before.

At 7pm that evening we all gathered in the teaching room in preparation for the séance. David spoke to us for quite a time before Christine took over to give us instructions as to what was expected of us.

1. To sing along enthusiastically – even if you don't know the words –'lah lah' it and particularly the second one which is an Irish jig – an audition for River Dance but with the mouth, not hands and feet – no clapping.

2. To join hands with the person next to you whenever she told us to – which was whenever any phenomena was about to happen and keep hold until it had finished.

3. To keep as still as possible and feet in close to your chair which is normal in other circles I've sat in.

Two independent checkers, one man and one woman, were selected.

Their job was to:

1. Check the séance room, cabinet and chair and its bindings that secure David's arms and legs, the length of material that is used as a gag, the 'trumpet' and its bag, the luminous plaque, drumsticks, harmonica, and a horn.

2. Do a body check on him, Christine and the two other circle members who had travelled to be there.

3. Select and check the strength of the large cable ties which were to be used to secure the fastenings on the bindings and the gag and the smaller ones which secure the buttonholes of the cardigan once David has buttoned himself into it with the buttons down the front.

Having removed all belts and jewellery, or taped over rings that could not be removed, to reduce any adverse interaction of the energy/ectoplasm with metals, we were all given a body check to make sure we were carrying nothing into the room.

The independent checkers carried out the checks on David and the circle members. The cardigan was secured and its ties through the buttonholes checked.

David was fastened into the chair and each fastening over bound with a cable tie then Christine gagged his mouth tightly and a cable tie was closed over the knot at the back of his neck. Finally, the curtains were dropped over the front of the cabinet.

This done the checkers took their places, one either side of the cabinet, the man next to Christine at the left of the cabinet (as we looked at it) and the woman next to Sarah, the circle member who was controlling the music player, on the right. The other visiting circle member sat amongst the rest of the sitters.

Now all was ready, the stand lamp by which the room had been lit was unplugged and placed outside the door, as too was the torch by which the binds had been checked in the cabinet. Robert then locked the door and sealed the blackout so the only light in the room was from the small luminous tabs on the CD player to enable Sarah to find the buttons.

After an opening prayer Christine called for the music and we sang, hummed, lah-lah-ed – whatever – with gusto to 'Search for the hero inside yourself', "do-did-do'd" to the Irish jig, joined in the bits we knew in 'True colours' and 'Somewhere over the Rainbow'. A great feeling of joy and laughter filled the room, at last we were there, and we were ready.

We heard a cultured voice speaking and Christine called for us to join hands which we did. It was William welcoming us all and after speaking for a while he called for questions and when someone asked a question he asked if he could approach them, walk over to them. We heard solid booted footsteps cross the floor and stand in front of them. He then asked if he could touch them and a large hand was then placed on their head – once or twice the person thought it was two hands as it was so large. Occasionally a cheek was stroked too. (David's hands are quite small.) Having answered the question, he returned to the cabinet and we were permitted to release hands, which was a relief as they were getting very sweaty. (August in Spain is not a good time for sitting in a séance).

It seemed to be no time before Timmy, the young boy, called for the trumpet which Christine placed in front of the cabinet and having joined hands again we were treated to an amazing light display from the luminous band on the large end as the trumpet was manipulated rapidly from one side of the room to the other. Looping and swirling, faster and further than I have witnessed before banging on the top of the cabinet and striking the blades of the overhead fan (stationary) and the ceiling. It came close to knees and heads, sometimes pausing to prod someone in the chest before it was away again – great fun, causing lots of laughter and again raising the vibrations to a new high. When the trumpet finished its acrobatics it was returned to Christine to be put back into its bag to hide the luminous band.

Timmy also went around the circle touching people and trying to separate their hands, prising apart fingers so they could feel his tiny fingers. Robert described them as being as small as his 5-year-old granddaughter's fingers and there was certainly no one as small as that in the room that night.

It was now time for personal contacts and to my delight Timmy asked if there was an 'Ann'. I replied there was and he told me he had two very important people coming for me and one of them was a very big Indian so he couldn't say no because he was frightened of him.

But first there was another man... I was told to encourage him to give the vibration for him to be able to draw close, and I am familiar with that because of all the years I have sat with Stewart Alexander.

Faintly, I heard a familiar husky 'Ann...' and I called to him, so he had my vibration and direction. I heard him walking haltingly towards me, my lovely Tom – just ten months since he passed over. I believe he found it difficult because of the emotion of being together again as he said to me, 'I always was sensitive.' – (he did easily become emotional – especially in the film 'Ghost'). Then, having placed his hands on either side of my head, he kissed me on the forehead. I could feel his familiar long fingers as he held me.

He released me and, hearing Robin Foy's voice, walked across the room to speak to Robin and Robert who were sitting directly opposite me. As he went his voice became stronger and more like his own normal voice, so much so that one lady from Switzerland – who has watched his video about five times – said was definitely recognisable as Tom Harrison, and this was backed up by Barbara, whom, with Robert, we have known since 2002 – so they know Tom well.

Tom returned to the cabinet and we heard the gurgling sound made as the ectoplasm dematerialises and reforms. Almost instantly I heard heavy footsteps coming towards me and felt in front of me a tall pillar of cold energy, and from above my head came Sunrise's special greeting to me – "My Little Sister". He then went on to say something in his own language which translated as "The Spirit is amongst you and around you." To have this special privilege of having my love and our special friend there in front of me was almost overwhelming. We could hear the steps as he made his way back to the cabinet and dematerialised.

Timmy then asked for Lynne or Linda. There was only a Lynne, sitting directly opposite the cabinet. Her father wished to come and speak to her.

This is her report:

This was my first experience of sitting in this type of séance. I had been well versed as to what could happen and was looking forward to it.

The checking of the people taking part was thorough as was that of the tie restraints, the clothing, and the chair of our medium David Thompson.

The evening was full of the most amazing spiritual characters. They spoke in varying different voices with intelligence but also with a strong sense of humour. My own father came through, he reminded me of a rabbit I had when I was young and I instantly remembered it. His voice was like I remembered it, firm but gentle although at first it was a little rasping. He told me that I was his "special little girl" which is what he used to call me when I was very young. He told me that he loved me and was proud of me. He cradled my face in both hands and kissed me on my forehead. I was talking back to him all the time calling him Dad like I used to.

It was without doubt a life changing moment, being made more memorable as my father and I had very little time together when he was alive.

The whole experience was one of total love and energy from every person and spirit present. I will never forget it.

Lynne Jones 24/08/2011

A wonderful, harmonious night.

In the Wednesday séance two more ladies had personal encounters. The first had her grandfather and spirit guide build together and both stand in front of her at the same time to speak to her. This was a 'first' for the Circle of the Silver Cord.

The second lady had her father come to her and when she couldn't remember a particular incident he told her that she always was scatterbrained, which she admitted was very evidential, as it was the sort of unjustified remark he would make.

This is part of what she wrote to me:

I was so excited when Timmy, who encourages and helps spirits to come through, called my name out saying there was someone for me who seemed to be my father! Before I knew it, I heard my father's voice about a foot in front of my face, talking to me from 'thin air'. It was my father's voice, unmistakeably. It actually sounded just like him! I knew he found it hard to come through and use the ectoplasm which I gather is hard for most people to use for the first time coming from the spirit world, but I kept encouraging him and he did a wonderful job of talking to me - his voice getting stronger and not only that but his character came through so well that he even managed to push one of my 'buttons' like he did on this side years ago! He talked to me about three evidential things... one was something way back in my childhood that I eventually remembered though I had wished at the time that he'd asked me something more recent. Then he spoke to me about his mother regarding something that was a major hallmark of his whole life and supplied one of the most important missing pieces of a jigsaw for me (too long and personal to describe here) which was also something that I could verify later, independently, and then he told me how much he liked the paintings I'd been creating, also incredibly evidential, because for the week before the séance, in every spare moment I'd had over that previous week, I'd been creating some artwork and it was something I hadn't done in several years now ... so it was very evidential all round.

In fact not to put too fine a point on it, it blew my mind, and along with saying I missed him, and him saying he missed me, I was even more gobsmacked when I felt his two hands take hold of my head and plant an emphatic, real kiss on my forehead with his lips, that the whole séance room must have heard!

After that the energy went and he left, to the sound of gurgling ectoplasm which is a hallmark sound of physical séances, leaving me absolutely amazed to have been able to have a one to one talk with my 'departed' father. It's an experience that left me with such certainty about the spirit world and life ongoing there, it was fantastic, specially as I'd not had the opportunity to be around this kind of thing for a very long time. I feel very lucky indeed to have been able to have this experience. I feel truly exhilarated. Almost like having been on the most incredibly 'holiday' to another planet.

Louisa Livingstone

On both of the evenings that I sat, Quentin Crisp also came and entertained us with his smooth repartee and walking over to Robert McLernon on the Monday night, told him he had a transvestite friend with him who wanted to speak to Rob. It was, to Rob's great delight, his guide 'George' – a flamboyant transvestite, who asked that he now be called 'Georgina'. Rob declared it, 'Brilliant' – so infrequently does a trance medium have the chance to physically speak to their own guides. Then on the Wednesday evening some long-stemmed roses had been brought by Bill, the other Silver Cord Circle member, to be given to ladies in the séance. Quentin took one from the vase on the floor between Christine and the cabinet, and gave it to Dawn who was directly opposite the cabinet and a second rose was placed in the lap of Barbara, our hostess for the week.

Again, on both the Monday and Wednesday evenings, the séances closed with the medium and his chair being levitated out of the cabinet and across the room to land some three metres in front of the cabinet. It landed with such a crash I thought some of the new tiles might have cracked.

On the second occasion they brought David out of trance before they did it. William asked for the gag to be removed before they brought him out of trance. Christine crossed the room with the key from the checker so that Rob could unlock the door to get the torch. The two checkers stood at the cabinet with the torch, watching as Christine eased the gag from between his lips and left it around his neck. They then returned to their seats, the torch was put outside and the door relocked before David was brought out of trance. We heard David say from within the cabinet, "I hate it when they do this." We heard a small thud, which I suspect was David's head against the cabinet top, before there was a loud crash and a scraping noise and David told us the chair was still moving.

The séance was now closed, and the door unlocked for Robert to retrieve the light. Once we had illumination we could see David and his chair were indeed about three metres from the cabinet. The independent checkers were called to inspect the binds; to note that the cable ties were still in place, the buckles of the arm straps and securing David's legs to the chair legs. The cardigan was now on back to front with all the ties still in place. The wire cutters which had been in the pocket of the male checker throughout the séance were now swiftly used to cut the ties so that the buckles could be undone and the cardigan removed.

David was still in a very sensitive state, having been more than one and a half hours in trance, and noise was kept to a minimum until he had left the room for a welcome cup of tea. Then you can imagine the chatter that erupted in the room at the wonderful contact we had all had.

Thursday saw a day of relaxing, sunbathing and exploring until the evening when David and Christine demonstrated their mental communication skills and a number of very detailed links were given, constrained a little in their flow by the recipients language difficulties.

And, of course, Tom finding he had a good link with Christine, having already made himself known to her in Australia, decided to close the evening of clairvoyance by giving her lots of snippets about himself of which she could know nothing – even to the rum we used to put in our hot chocolate every morning, finishing the evening with laughter. It was a good, if emotional, evening.

On Friday evening in the séance, having earlier asked a question of William about language in the spirit world, Katya's grandfather built and spoke to her in German, her first language.

This is what she wrote to me:

> With the help of another Spirit helper "Jack" my Granddad managed to speak to me in German... He said "mein Liebling" various times which means "my darling" and "das ist wunderbar" which means "this is wonderful" - unfortunately his voice was very quiet and I couldn't get it all but Spirit Jack took over after my Granddad couldn't stay any longer and said to me, "Your Grandfather says he is your Geistfuehrer, whatever a Geistfuehrer is, do I know what a Geistfuehrer is," and he walked away from me mumbling about the word Geistfuehrer..... I then explained that Geistfuehrer simply means "guide" in English.... Later the lady who sat next to me confirmed that she understood German and it was audible to her as well....
>
> Katja Symons

I doubt that David knew many German words and certainly not to converse as the communicator did.

As many have said, with the checks that were in place, no-one could move without others knowing – we had spirit there in that place and individuals had specific evidence that no one could have known.

The week was alive with love and we can only thank Robin and Sandra Foy for the input they have had in the organization, together with Robert and Barbara for opening their Centre to the world, coping with sensitive people, and achieving a dream not only for themselves but for so many to come together from across the world.

Thank you and we look forward to the next visit.

* * * * *

166

Three months later we had a visit by another physical medium, Scott Milligan.

Tom and I had met and sat with Scott, back in 2004 and saw what promise he showed then. Now at the Acacia Centre I was to see how this young man had developed. Early in his introductory talk Scott told us he had once asked his mentor, John, what a spiritual person was like, and John had told him to look at Tom Harrison. Tom would not have considered himself such but besides being very human and down to earth that was the effect he had on many people.

Besides encouraging those attending the weekend to develop their trance state, we were to see the phenomena created through Scott's own physical mediumship.

In the séance on the Saturday evening we witnessed many different types of phenomena including, in red light, seeing streams of ectoplasm coming from him and piling on the floor. We heard voices speaking through a voice box some distance away from the medium. Towards the end of the séance, when the voice box had been operating for some time, Daniel, the child guide of the circle, speaking from the centre of the room, several metres from Scott in the cabinet, said, "I don't usually do this but the voice box has dried up and so I will try to relay what they want to say." The person wasn't named nor to whom they wanted to speak, but Daniel started to ask questions to which I could answer yes until he came to–

Daniel. Did he like cheese? (*Ann.* Not particularly, but I do.) I can see him going to the cheese counter.

Ann. Yes – I bought 3 packs at Iceland two days ago.

Daniel. There are some photos of him. He needs you to get out the ones of him when he looked his best and have them made larger.

Here it is – the photo I see everyday, taken two months after we were married in 1998.

Something strange occurred at the end of the séance, that none of us had experienced before. The tiled floor was

Tom Harrison

covered in moisture, like a dew. It was extremely wet and slippery, but the wooden walls of the room and the wooden sides of the cabinet were dry. Daniel had told us the voice box had 'dried up' and couldn't be manipulated but we had all this moisture. – Weird! There is so much we do not understand in physical phenomena.

* * * * *

The following February (2012) we had Kai Muegge visit the Centre from Germany.

This was a Festival of Firsts

• It was the first visit of Kai Muegge to the Acacia Centre in Spain.

• The first time he had used a cabinet that was not his own.

• It was the first time that photographs, yet to be published on Kai's website, of ectoplasm being extruded in white light had been shown to the 'public'.

• It was the first time through his mediumship that ectoplasm was seen in good white torchlight and a face visible to most of the sitters, was seen impressed into the mass of ectoplasm against the curtain of the cabinet.

On Tuesday morning, February 7th, fifteen of the final eighteen delegates assembled at the Acacia Centre of Robert and Barbara McLernon in the Murcia region of Spain. As well as a number of the regulars at the centre, visitors had flown in from Madrid, USA, Australia and UK for this third festival of physical mediumship. Very few of us were known to Kai and his fiancée Julia before this meeting but we were quickly to become friends. The morning was taken up with introductions and a time of getting to know each other.

After lunch we were treated to a talk by Robin Foy, one of the organisers, on Leslie Flint, the Direct Voice medium, with whom Robin had sat a number of times.

At 5pm we gathered for the introductory talk as to what we might expect in the séance which was to follow. Following that introduction Kai left us and we were frisked before entering the séance room. When we were ready Robin carried out a strip search of Kai before he brought him to the special séance room in the garden of the Centre. Assuring us that nothing was hidden in his clothes nor on his person.

The number of sitters for each séance was restricted to eighteen at the request of the spirit team.

Each evening started with such loud raps and hammerings around the room particularly on the roof – so loud you would have thought we had a team of joiners repairing it.

Although the Felix Experimental Group (FEG) is not known for giving many personal 'survival' connections, – in Germany, we are told, they are more interested in 'phenomena' but not in 'personal proof of survival' However the approach was adjusted for us.

One of the early happenings of that first evening was the materialisation of a man within the horseshoe of sitters described by Hans Bender, the control of the medium and leader of the team of chemists that oversees the phenomena, as – 'tall, ninety-two when he went and part of the British spiritualist movement'.

Who else could it be but Tom Harrison, my husband, back again in his 'home' Centre. We heard his familiar shuffling footsteps as he moved across the room. Professor Bender then went on to say the man wished to touch someone in the circle. Because I was at almost the furthest possible point (almost 3metres) from the cabinet I encouraged him to try to touch Barbara who was nearer but no, with an extreme effort, I felt a tap firmly on my knees (a warm, soft but firm fist) before he was pulled back towards the cabinet. A few minutes later, after we had sung again, Hans Bender came back to say that the man, 'Thomas', wanted to tell that lady that he was very proud of her and Bender said he believed 'he used to be in a circle' (so true – several).

That evening we also had instruments being tapped, shaken, moved. We saw fingers against an illuminated plaque over two metres away from the cabinet and coming from different directions – not from the direction of the cabinet. We felt touches. I felt as though an owl's wing had moved across my knees. Barbara felt she had an animal on her knee. We had been warned that these ideo-plastic formations can occur.

So very different from what we, in UK circles, normally have.

At the insistence of the spirit control, Kai was put under the control of Julia and Sandra Foy, who were sitting either side of him, whenever the movement of objects or formation of hands was occurring in the room as no straps or restraints are used. This was by each placing one hand on his leg nearest to them and held his hands with their other hands and assure us that Kai was not moving. Occasionally Sandra was asked to reach across and check that Julia was still holding him too.

In the latter part of the two-hour long séance we watched ectoplasm being pulled from the medium's mouth – by the medium– in a good red light. We had been told that it would be a sticky substance. This it certainly appeared to be, adhering to the medium's fingers but he continued to pull it from his mouth and to pull it apart with his fingers to show us the fibrous gossamer-like structure of spiders' webs threads in the mass of an unstructured web, like the ones I have seen in my garden in Spain.

Towards the end of this demonstration the fingers of Kai's right hand appeared to rub the ectoplasm, working it to reveal a tiny Buddha form – an apport which was a gift to the Acacia Centre, which, Julia told us, although it had come from this sticky mass, as she was given it was dry, hot and clean.

On the second day Kai told us of the wealth of historical evidence of Physical Mediumship supported by many historic photographs.

On Thursday afternoon, in the second séance, Robert felt a very large spider crawling up his leg and body to his chest before it disappeared – another ideo-plastic form. We told him it was because he had teased Barbara about a snake coming.

Two people were touched from behind and both, being mediums, knew that it had been their mothers. Bender said he would try to get confirmation of the people, but we didn't get it as the séance was interrupted by the sitter next to me being taken ill and who had to leave the room. Unfortunately, we removed her chair and that disturbed the energy matrix.

We were able to re-start when they had 'rebuilt' the matrix in which they work. After that the trumpet moved around the room, conducting the singing. Then it rested on Robert's arm and he was told by the control to take hold of it. It played 'hard to get' for a few seconds before letting him hold it and they then had a tug of war. Robert told us that the pull was extremely strong and the sitter next to him could feel Rob's chair moving with the force of holding it. We watched luminous ping-pong balls being moved on a tray and tossed on to the floor two landing nearby, over two metres from the cabinet.

Julia was told to switch on the red light and Sandra and Julia held back the cabinet curtains. We then watched ectoplasm being extracted from the medium in a good red light (full 40watt brightness). Once the ectoplasm had been disconnected from the medium (Yes, they do do that in this circle) a hand and arm pushed upwards in it from a pile on the floor and the hand waved to us! Hans Bender told us it was his arm. Then the curtains were closed briefly.

After re-forming, the curtains were opened again and we watched a column of ectoplasm, about 6″ (15cm) across, grow to head height just within the front of the cabinet, with the red light on it all the time – just as Tom must have seen when his Aunt Agg built for the first time in his mother's circle back in 1947.

Friday was a day off for our visiting medium and we had a fun day exploring the basics of dowsing followed in the afternoon by tiptology (table tilting), a method employed by our pioneers to communicate with the spirit world – more of that in Chapter 22.

On Saturday afternoon, in our third sitting, as well as touches (for me, in my hair, from behind), we saw hands in silhouette against a plaque, the instruments were shaken and tapped to the music. Then we were treated to the experiment which the controls of Rudy Schneider would do – a handkerchief with luminous spots on the corners was taken, by an unseen psychic rod, from the outstretched fingers of two different sitters and we watched it float around the room like a jellyfish even going beyond the circle over my head (this time I was sitting nearer the cabinet).

I had experienced this the previous year when on a visit to Hans Schaer's Finca in Ibiza, together with Kai's FEG circle and other visitors. On that occasion I was given the handkerchief to hold out at arm's length and to keep hold until the psychic rod with a gripper on the end had good hold of it and was tugging it from my grasp. Unfortunately, I let go when I felt the tug and the hold wasn't strong enough and it fell to the floor. Ken, the sitter next to me, was more successful in holding on to it and I could see the glow on the psychic rod from the reflected light of the spots on the handkerchief.

More personal connections were given to the sitter from USA, when a patient of his came back to thank him for his help in passing over. Also his guide, a Sioux Indian medicine man, a guide in their circle, came to speak to him and gave the Lakota word meaning 'medicine man' (which he knew) as well as other information. We could hear the feet pattering against the tiled floor as Bender passed on the information. The sitter assured us later, that he had not mentioned that he was a doctor and no one knew the Lakota word and its connection with him.

A lady sitter was given a contact from a guide who comes to her when she is writing music, which gave her a great boost in confidence.

Hans Bender also asked for a message to be passed on to lady named 'Morgana??' We replied, 'Morag', he told us she was right and gave also the name of Walter and described the man. Morag was not present that evening, but she had told us that she felt the presence of her father on the Thursday evening, as she wanted to whistle during the singing, and Hans was confirming that she was correct and the other man he described, very accurately, was her husband's uncle – an excellent connection.

Towards the end of the séance the red light, again full 40watt exposure, showed us the ectoplasm streaming from Kai's mouth, with him pulling it out. This time it looked like cotton wool – not sticky – across his knee and on to the floor and again he pulled it open with his hands to show us the internal gossamer thread structure. Julia was instructed to turn off the light and then within seconds to put it on again and it was all gone – reabsorbed into the etheric body – we were told.

Bender then asked Julia if she trusted them. Very tentatively she replied, 'Yes.'

"You do not sound sure."

"I thought you might be asking me a question."

"Well do you trust us?"

This time, more firmly, she said, "Yes, I do."

He then went on to ask her to get the torch (US-flashlight) with white light and shine it on to the floor by her feet. She was then to

A lamp similar to this

slowly move the light up on to the cabinet and up the curtain. As she did so we could see Kai's face poking through the opening of the cabinet curtain and from his nose were 'ropes' of ectoplasm which then looped round into a mass of looser ectoplasm, seemingly attached to the cabinet curtain to the medium's right side, several inches away from his face. Bender asked if we could see a face in the ectoplasm – and told us it was his face. From my position in the circle I could not see it clearly as it was turned slightly away from my side of the circle but most of the others could. It was held for quite some seconds before Julia was asked to turn the light out.

This must be the first time that white light has been shone on to ectoplasm for many, many years. The light was quite bright too and only approximately two feet from it. The lamp was the sort you use as a bicycle front light.

They were amazing séances, so much light and openness.

A wonderful five days of variety and contact. Variety in music too, using different music each evening as, and this was stressed to us by Hans Bender, it is the sound of our voices which is important and we had to be able to sing along with it, joyfully.

* * * * *

In September of that year David Thompson returned to do a second week. This time there was more concentration on teaching, particularly on development of trance for the delegates. Nationalities were as widespread as before, but included this time a family from Ukraine. They spoke very little English but with their interpreter translating we were able to make them very welcome. It seemed that they were desperate to make contact with their son who had died very suddenly.

At one point during the first sitting things were quite disturbed but eventually settled down, and the rest of the evening flowed as in the previous year. However on the second evening a spokesman for the spirit team explained that the young man who had come for the family from Ukraine had made attempt to reach them and that had been the cause of the upset. They told us that they were going to help him make the contact with the assistance of one of David's spirit team 'May' – the Afro-Caribbean member of the spirit team.

The family were sitting just two seats away from me so I was able to work out what was happening. With the support of 'May', the materialised form of the young man was able to move across the floor, to hold the hands of his young wife and his parents, and to talk to them in their own language. It was quite a short but very emotional reunion, and he did extremely well to be able to hold the form on this first occasion—and I might add we were all very emotional and happy that this had been possible. I know it made the evening, for this is the real purpose of physical mediumship and circles.

Later in the sitting the luminous plaque was taken out of its bag and starting at the left hand side of the circle the sitters there, including my friend Kate, were able to see the blob of ectoplasm turn into a hand against the brightly lit board. Slowly the plaque moved around the room stopping before many of the sitters and a voice from the darkness invited them to touch the hand. One sitter exclaimed that it had fingernails to which the voice responded "Why wouldn't I have fingernails?"

I was seated about two-thirds of the way round the circle and when it approached me I found that the plaque was placed high up under my chin so that the fingers almost touched my skin. It remained there for quite some time and when I asked "Why are you doing that?" the voice replied, "For a very special reason." He then asked if I wanted to touch it which I did of course, finding it firm and strong, just as Walter's had been some seventeen years before. – I realised later I should have asked what that reason was.

* * * * *

These were amazing opportunities for so many people who had never sat in a physical circle before and to witness so much that I had had the privilege of adding my energy and experience to.

174

Post script

In the week before David's second visit to Spain I had taken the opportunity of flying over to England for the wonderful international gathering of physical mediums in Eastbourne.

There I was able to witness José Medrado paint in the style of the Impressionist masters in spirit, completing paintings in just 5-7 minutes and they were amazingly like the style of their paintings. The artists in spirit had agreed to work with him, providing all the money raised from the sale of his paintings went to support his charity work in Brazil.

In the séance with Scott Milligan I was again fortunate to have contact with Tom. Quietly but distinctly towards the end of the séance we heard a voice say, 'Annnn...' It was Tom speaking through the voice box, telling me he wanted to have the first dance with me but not for some time! This was a reference to our 'village' 'Street Party' in Spain the previous Friday. Tom and I had danced at it every year and was the first time that I had gone to it without him – but I had danced with some of my women friends.

There was other personal evidence but this was the best:

Tom told me he had done something for me – written a message. "I didn't know I could do that. ... Catch my two kisses."

And I heard the sound of two kisses being sent.

At the end of the sitting on one of the sheets of A4 paper, which Sue Farrow had initialled before the séance began, was written –

Tom... With x always. xx

And why two kisses?

– That day was the 19th Anniversary of the day he first kissed me, on the weekend that we met – and yes – that day it had been two kisses.

Spirit writing – a message from Tom.

Tiptology – Table-turning and Communication

The pioneers' methods of communication are still valid in today's world. Nothing, I think, can give more fun to dedicated sitters and spirit children than having a table rock, wriggle, dance or whirl around in response to singing, or questions when they are unable to speak audibly from the spirit world. To move to a recipient and then respond to questions or spell out the answers may give great comfort or even open a door to more investigation and perhaps the development of verbal communication.

As I have already described in Chapter 6 we had a wonderful time in the Circle in West Yorkshire with the dining table responding in so many ways which meant they could talk to us and it certainly raised the energies to enable further development. One evening one of the spirit children told us she wanted a 'party' later. So following the sitting we sat in the lounge area with the small baize topped card table and very quickly it was on the move and dancing all around the room, rocking out different rhythms to which we sang along when we recognised the tune. Everything from 'Knees up Mother Brown' to 'Rock around the Clock'. As Tom had brought the video camera with him he was able to record it as we, with much laughter, danced/chased around the room with our fingertips touching the table top.

One evening we took a new friend of ours to a Noah's Ark sitting at a community hall near Rotherham in Yorkshire with Stewart as the medium. It was John's first sitting and not only did the trumpet move very close to him during the sitting but Christopher also brought family contacts for him. As so often happens, his mind went blank and he was unable to place them. Also at the sitting was the medium from our Saturday Circle and when we introduced him to her after the séance she immediately invited us to go home with her.

Having been introduced to the family and a cup of tea enjoyed, the cups were removed from the small card table and following a short opening prayer, we proceeded to show him our link to the spirit world using that same table.

This is Tom's report of the evening:

Report of events, 24th April 1996 at 10.45pm

The green baize topped card table responded to our touch immediately. After much hectic movement in time to our singing it was asked if there was someone there who wanted to give a message – "YES" it rocked (our signals were one rock for 'yes' and stillness for 'no', to save energy) So Ann did her stuff as Alphabet lady.

"H-A-R-O..."   P--- asked if it was Harold   "YES"

What P--- -did not know was that at Stewart's public sitting earlier that evening Christopher had given John a "Harold" whom he had known in a 'big building'. John acknowledged the Harold but couldn't think of the big building. Christopher said he kept chickens – Yes, agreed John. Then Christopher had asked if E. meant anything to John – he couldn't immediately accept it, and the circle was closed as the power had gone.

Back to Tom's report –

John asked if the building was at the end of a jetty "No". Could you please spell out where the building was H-O-S-P- ... "Hospital? 'Yes' it rocked.

John then told us that was where Harold had died. (Later, travelling home in the car, he told us that Harold was his father.)

Ann asked, "Is there anyone else there?" "Yes." Ann slowly spelt out the alphabet ... On responding to "E" the table rocked over on to John's knees.

John asked then could it be his daughter, Elizabeth? The table went "bananas" with excitement. (In Stewart's séance John had gone blank about the E. but was so pleased now.)

His daughter had been at boarding school in UK while John was in Hong Kong and she passed over very suddenly within 24 hours with a virulent 'Flu which had been a tremendous shock to John and his wife.

E. was asked if she had a message and she spelled out "O-K" and again rocked the table on to John's knees, pressing it there as though hugging him. Then we got "H-A-P-" and P--- said "Happy?" YES – with more vigorous rocking.

John asked if it was Elizabeth who had thumped on their wardrobe door during the night three weeks after her passing which awakened him but not his wife. John had felt it was her and that she was happy. She confirmed this with more excited table movements.

The table had moved from one side of the room, where P--- and Tom were sitting, to the other to John, for the communication with John, so as A--- a was about to close the session she asked if Grey Wolf was there and the table responded "Yes" – to which A---a casually said that it had better move the table back to where it had started – and it pirouetted across the room with just very slight contact from A---a and Ann!"

What Tom did not say in this report that the table was under the light touch of J--- , A---a and me throughout the whole contact.

One of our table sessions which we called 'A Party for the children' while we were at Brayton near Selby.

Fast forward now to 2012, to the Friday of Kai's visit to the Acacia Centre when he and Julia had a day off. We had a number of tables of various sizes height, and shapes, but I stuck to my own card table made by my father in the 1930s.

We did not attempt to spell out the alphabet to communicate but we, and we assume the spirit children, had lots of fun moving the tables. We had five tables available for the session and we very quickly had most of them, rocking spinning and whizzing around the room – in full daylight with sun pouring through the windows. Ours invaded the kitchen and pinned me against the kitchen sink! before dancing out again and playing 'tig' with another table – stopping within two inches of each other – whilst we sang Nursery Rhymes and other joyful songs. The control was amazing!

In the vigorous movement my card table, (*see right*) made by my father in 1930s, folded itself up, so we had to stick insulating tape around the rod – that controlled the legs – to the top to prevent it collapsing again. We were weak with laughter at the end of it all.

Tom had told me on the previous Sunday, through Robert's mediumship during the service, that he would move the table and had given me the trigger song to do that. Towards the end of the afternoon, we all sat in a double circle with my card table in the centre, trying to get it to levitate. As the energy was fading, I started to sing 'Half a pound of tu'penny rice....' – the trigger. Immediately the table became energised and spun wildly around, pirouetting on one leg for some minutes with only the lightest of touches from some of the six people in contact. Both Barbara and I could sense Tom's presence and so could one of the other sitters who had known Tom years before, but did not know of his promise for this week. We had great difficulty in keeping contact to allow the table to spin under our fingers.

A wonderful experience.

That Nursery rhyme was the opening song every week for the circle in West Yorkshire and which was the trigger then for the table to start to move.

For those not familiar with the rhyme:

"Half a pound of tu'penny rice,
Half a pound of treacle,
That's the way the money goes
Pop goes the weasel."

Following their experience during Kai's week, two of our regular Acacia Circle sitters asked if they could do more development with the table. It was decided eventually that my table was the most convenient to work with because of its height (less back breaking) and the top size (how many could stand/sit round it.)

With the tape still in place we sat in the dark, in the large room which had been used for the séances, and it was not long before the table, with four pairs of hands lightly on it, was racing around the room while Rob was still sitting at the entrance to the cabinet (in trance).

We did eventually get it calmed down and had several sittings where family members communicated with us.

Shortly before we had started the sittings, I was editing an edition of Anabela Cardoso's *ITC Journal* for publication, in which there was an article from Canada describing the communications they had had through a table by asking questions. I had never heard of this method. I was only familiar with the Alphabet method. I was highly sceptical as to how accurate it could be, and then, I found myself thrown into doing exactly that.

The first time we had this sort of communication was at the end of May, just three months after the seminar. These are my notes from the recording:

Katja felt there was movement in the table before the prayer was said so we had to tell her not to put her hands on until we had opened. The table was then still until Rob asked, 'Is there anybody there?'

From then on the table moved non-stop – except when implying 'NO' when it was quite still. When it started moving, we asked if it was someone who'd been before – 'NO'.

It then moved towards Scott (Rob's son) and pushed into him, and he asked if it was his Gran (Mary Agnes) it rocked wildly (as in delight). The table moved back slightly then settled into a tick-tock rhythm. I asked Scott if there was a special clock belonging to his Gran – 'YES' – (he told us it had been repaired but it was still in his brother's car.) The table moved right up to Scott in a 'cuddle'.

Scott remarked he would have thought the sound of horses would be with his Gran and the table rhythm changed to a galloping horse sound with an extra click sound between the tick-tock (sort of clipetty-clipetty). (*Much laughter!*)

Another week we had trance communication as well, when Rob went into trance quite early.

At five minutes in, 'John Pritchard' made his presence known and spoke briefly saying he did not think much of the song (Hey Jude) but he did appreciate the music as Mr. Lennon was present. J.P. told us he was still trying to move the bells (the wind chimes attached to the ceiling fan). He wanted to let us know he was there. Katja said she had felt a strong pull on her Solar Plexus when he said that and he told her 'Patience.' (another of our songs).

The table then went into sounds mode and produced the scraping sound which John Pritchard said was rather like a saw. I asked if it was someone I would know (My father who made the table). We heard J.P. say 'Oh, dear!'as the sound then became uneven like a saw used badly. I had used a very rusty saw to cut the end of a broom handle to repair it three days earlier, and I'm not good at using a saw, even when sharp. The table responded by making the sound of hammering – which I'd had to do to get the handle back in. Showing that they had been around. So good to know – I do ask for their help!

A month later we had an amazing contact. Many of our sittings involved clairvoyance or more particularly claircognisance and clairsentinence – a knowing/ feeling and this happened this evening, together with table responses. In this next transcript I have added the time to give you an idea of the patience that is needed sometimes.

12.20min Debbie sensed the name 'William'.

14.00min. The table then moved across to me turning so the open side could move right in against me (and not knock the knees – in a cuddle) I established it was Tom and that it was good to be back. The table began to move vigorously again and as the tune finished it tipped right over away from me.

20.20 I felt as though a pin was stuck into my ring finger. Quite sharp.

25.50 Barbara got a terrific pain on the right side of her head. She felt a soldier close to her (*shuddered*) and thought WWII.

26.30 Rob felt Archie very prominent, at that the table responded and confirmed he was. It took off as though tap-dancing, rocking faster and faster. Then rocking slowly and scraping, but not sawing.

29min – 34min. Everyone became very quiet, I found it difficult to respond when Barbara spoke, saying I had tremendous pressure on the back of my head. Barbara had pressure all down her right side. The table was close in by Barbara and me all this time unmoving.

34.40 'Island of Dreams' was the next song. We could sing again. Barbara said she kept asking for them to take the pain away but it kept coming back... I said there must be a reason – 'Who is it ?'

38.15 Barbara asked me, "Did Tom have a friend in WWI?" That surprised her because she had initially thought WWII. She had tried to correct it but I said, "Yes he did, his namesake. That's the William."

The table rocked to tap loudly ...'YES'

Barbara. That's what Debbie had.

Ann. Yes, that's Tom's second name.

The table went 'mad' – rocking in approval.

Ann. Is it Willie? Willie Earle really?

The table continued to rock and bang, with that Barbara had a blast of cold air over her and I felt it across my shoulders (It had not been cold before even from the fan).

Ann. Oh Fantastic, Brilliant! (I felt a strong pressure on my head) I told them that I thought it was July that he passed, just before the end of the war.

Ann. It's lovely to have you here. Have you met up with Tom? He'll be so pleased. The table moved again to knock. 'YES'.

I said I had thought of it as Tom's name when Debbie spoke. Barbara said when she thought about it, the uniform was from WWI. Tom was definitely there and that was what the confusion was, as Tom was in WWII.

I told them Willie died a very short time before Tom was born. and Tom's father added the 'William' in memory of a young man he had tried to take care of in the trenches.

Rob had a campanologist with him but we couldn't place one. (Possibly Pritchard as he's always trying to ring our chimes.)

Barbara could see a young soldier. She knew it was a head wound. He worked in the trenches to help others pass over.

42.50 I asked if the other 'William' was there as well? (Brittain Jones) to which the table responded – and added 'and the rest of the circle.?' – more energetic movement. Tom's Mam's circle was there.

Ann. 'Great'.

We went on to question William Earle. He is not working in the trenches now but works with Tom, not in healing, but with a circle.

Barbara and Rob had been getting the head pain all week and the table confirmed William had been with them. Rob asked if he would take the table to whom he wanted to work with. The table moved right into Barbara.

45.15 The table tipped over towards Katja on two legs and then on to one leg it then came back down and tapped.

46 .00 We sensed Tom had taken over and when Rob asked if he was going to work with anyone in the circle the table was still. – a 'NO'.

I said 'You are too busy working in another circle.' the table was again still – 'NO'.

So amid laughter Barbara said that was a joke wasn't it at which there was a lot of vigorous movement and banging.

Rob. You are never going to leave this circle are you? The table was still. – 'NO'.

Barbara. Definitely not. Thank you for bringing William – more vigorous, extended table movement.

What a fantastic session.

On a more personal level, the following week, at the end of an evening of a McLernon family reunion, when the energy changed, and the table moved to me, it was Tom. The table banged hard against my knee.

Barbara asked if he was coming to visit the David Thompson seminar again this year – a strong response saying – 'YES'.

Barbara then asked me if I had done something with the chair Tom used to sit in. I have recently cleaned it and covered it, and the matching one as well, with the yellow throws from the guest room. 'YES', it responded. I do sit in his chair also because he told me to. *(and the table nudged into me in a mini cuddle).*

The table started moving in a rocking figure of eight. Barbara thought it was like a dance and a letter S was 'danced' – 'YES'.

I immediately knew it was to do with the Street Party in mid-September, which I am unsure about attending because we always danced there, together, and I felt the memories still raw. – When I explained this to them, the table gave a very strong movement. – 'YES'.

Barbara. You don't want to miss it do you, Tom?

This was met with a <u>strong</u> response from the table as though dancing, meaning he wanted to be there.

I told them it had been on my mind but found it difficult because we always had such good dancing there. There was strong movement by the table – and the table went to give Debbie and Katja a 'cuddle' – as he always did when in the physical!

It then pinned Rob in his chair and finally came to me and I promised I'd get the ticket.

I closed the circle in prayer.

I did go to the street party and joined in the dancing with my female friends, imagining he was with me.

This four months of sitting showed me that the method of asking questions and receiving answers through the table movement could be as valid as the alphabet method.

I would add, however, a degree of awareness is a great help in knowing what to ask and to respond to images that might come into your mind.

Special Reunions and a Spirit Healing

As we had had no funeral for Tom I decided to have a memorial tree planting celebration for him, in the garden at Cober Hill, close to where Stewart had placed a bench for his sister Gaynor. There, in the April following Tom's passing, we planted an oak tree which Tom and I had grown from an acorn and which my brother had cared for over the past eleven years while we were in Spain. Among the guests were Eric and Jackie, our friends from York. Jackie was by then terminally ill with cancer but well enough to attend and the following evening be at one of Stewart's Circle sittings.

This sitting had been re-arranged so that Eric and Jackie and I could sit with them before I returned to Spain.

Within a few minutes of 'opening' the circle with a prayer, Tom came through and spoke with us through Stewart's trance.[1] The music had been quite loud but when Walter came through, he explained that the music energy had been necessary to help Tom to speak.

Walter began by giving me a warm welcome.

Ann. It is so good to be here.

Walter. It is so nice to be able to welcome you. It is like old times and in spite of the fact that Tom is not sitting with you – he is not there, in the physical, he is now – he has taken his place – in that special circle in my world where he works with you. (*Ann.* Yes.) He is very much here this evening. He did his utmost to speak and you know, Ann, how difficult it is for him. I think that it was an indication of the great love that he has for you all, but particularly for Ann of course. He did his utmost.

---

1. For details see *'Harrison Connections: Tom Harrison's desire to communicate'* (SNPP2014)

When I asked Walter if the hoarseness of Tom's voice was because of his physical condition that he still picks up, he told that it wasn't that, but the difficulty he was encountering in manipulating Stewart's vocal chords, as he was still having to use them rather than an independent method. It is exceedingly difficult, he said, to utter a single word – but in time. They had all had the same problem in their "early days".

He continued, "Even for we who speak with such clarity today – when we first came – when we first endeavoured to master this method of control – when we first tried to speak, it was a long time before we were able to speak with any clarity what-so-ever. It takes time and it takes patience. There are so many problems involved I cannot begin to tell you."

He then welcomed Eric and Jackie, and on hearing Katie's voice welcomed her also. He asked about the third part of her book[2], which we had been going through that afternoon as we prepared it for the printer. When I told him, this was his reply.

"Ann, perhaps even you do not fully appreciate the work that you have performed together. What you have accomplished these works will give great comfort to all who find them, read them and consider what is contained within. They are a lasting testament to all that takes place in this small room. You will reach many, many people, many folks in your world and perform a great service not only to your world but also to ours. A great truth of survival. We are all so appreciative..... Okay, okay."

Later Walter told us they had looked forward to this meeting for some time – particularly Tom. "He was so thrilled yesterday but of course we were all there we were all present. Ann, Gaynor is here also, as indeed she was yesterday ... We expect nothing less ... okay."

Ann. It was lovely that the gardeners had considered putting a tree in that corner and we were able to supply the tree.

Walter. Yes that was a plus, yes.

He left us with instructions to use the lower light when Stewart returned and move our chairs back to the wall. Unfortunately, as I moved our chairs the light of my recorder came on and although I

2 See *'Experiences of Trance and Physical Phenomena with the Alexander Circle Part 3'.* Now included in *'Touching the Next Horizon'* (SNPP books 2021)

tried sitting on it, Dr Barnett had to ask me to switch it off, as even that small amount of light was interfering with the proceedings. as they were "working with a material that was extremely light sensitive."

Dr Barnett came very quietly at first and asked for the volume of the music to be reduced so he could hear himself. He apologised as it may take some time before his voice would become audible to us all, but by then we could all hear it including Katie, as spirit team had constructed the 'hearing mechanism' to enable her to hear.

The voice suddenly strengthened and we heard him say: "I'm speaking in my own voice. I hope you can hear." (*June*. Oh we can. / *Ann*. Very clearly.) I would like if I may speak to the lady Jackie.

Jackie. Hello Dr Barnett.

Dr Barnett. Hello my dear. I'm so pleased – indeed I'm thrilled to find myself speaking with you once again. I want you to listen to what I have to say and I hope also that your husband ... may I call you Eric (*Eric*. You may.) Yes, and you may call me Dr Barnett. (*gentle laughter*) I want you also to listen to what I have to say now. *(Eric.& Jk*. Yes.) First of all we want you to be assured that we in our world are very close to you at all times therefore we are aware of your health situation. And I have to say I'm not speaking merely to you Jackie but I'm speaking also to Eric because I know what affects Jackie affects you in equal measure (*Eric*. Certainly.) and so many people tend to forget this that when a loved one suffers then all suffer. And you are extremely close the two of you and so please understand, that we understand. But Jackie I know that you have been sending out your thoughts to me each evening.

Jackie. Yes that's right.

Dr Barnett. And in return I have listened to you. I have listened to your thoughts, your very thoughts and because you have invited me in, it has allowed me to draw even closer and continue with the healing ministry. (*Jk*. Thank you.) but this evening I want to do something further. Firstly, however, I want to ask if you would kindly send your thoughts to me each evening (*Jk*. I certainly will.) I am pleased to hear that but this evening I would like to come to you and I would like to lay my hands upon you to see what I can do, with your permission of course. *(Jk*. Certainly, Dr Barnett.)

Eric. Does it help that I send my thoughts every evening as well?

Dr Barnett. Well, but of course, but of course. Because quite simply it creates an ambience, it creates an atmosphere of purity, ... purity of thought and this impinges itself up on your immediate atmosphere and this allows me to draw closer than I would otherwise be able to do. *(Eric.* I see.) So if you would all do that for me I would be grateful. And I want to reassure you Jackie if I may, and also you too, Eric, that everything is being done that can be done *(Jk. & E.* Thank you.) Be very positive in your outlook *(Jk.* I will.) and know that my world is close by always.

June. That's nice to know isn't it?

Jackie. It is.

Dr Barnett. What we do each evening is nothing to what we can do in person and because you are here then I will avail myself of the opportunity to come to you in person. *(Jk.* Thank you.)

June. That's nice Dr Barnett, that'll be lovely.

Dr Barnett. Can you all hear me? Because I feel that I'm speaking quite well.

June. You are speaking very well. – *(everyone joins in with comments.)*

Dr Barnett. I have to say something about the gentleman Tom whilst I'm here. It will not surprise you, Ann, that I have spent quite some time in his company. *(Ann.* Yes I should think you would have.) He is a man of such... he is so inquisitive. He wants to know and he wants to understand *(Ann.* Absolutely, yes.) and if I may say something to you I know that you are aware ... indeed I know that you are all aware when a soul passes from your world into mine but I want you to know this, that it would be impossible to convey to you the celebration which took place to welcome him into this world. *(Ann.* I understand so.) We have waited a long time and he is now reaping the rewards that he richly deserved. *(June.* That's lovely.) But, Ann, you have great work to do and you do not need me to tell you that. *(Ann.* I know.) You know, you know, just continue on as we all know that you will. You are in many ways in a fortunate position and because you have been so close to Tom that you have such a great understanding. You may not have witnessed what he witnessed all those years but my goodness he has enthused you over a long period of time. (*Ann.* Yes. it is seventeen years he's been training me.) Yes, a long time for you to continue on. As we know that you will.

It is always such a privilege for me and I know I speak for everyone on my side of life that to come here to communicate. It is. ... (*Ann.* It is lovely to hear you.)

As we uttered our thanks Dr Barnett responded with "There is no necessity. Believe me we enjoy these evening as much as you do....." Our comments drowned out his final words.

With that we saw the trumpet start to rise and it moved slowly towards me until it was about a foot away, it then circled round in small circles moving both ways. Sunrise was showing he was there. (*Ann.* Hello, my friend.) June then told me that he still came to the circle when we weren't there.

Ann. It's lovely to have you working. Are you going to speak through the trumpet again?

It moved towards Jackie. We then heard Walter say "I am still in control of the mechanism."

As it moved gently around the room Jackie commented that this was mind boggling, "What on earth is happening? You are used to it here but to me ... and the amount of work that must go into it."

It was the first time she had seen the trumpet move like this, whereas Eric was used to it in our circle at Brayton.

June. Absolutely fantastic it is.

Ann. Just this lovely control.

June. It is so mild and so.... *(the trumpet moved towards Katie)* It usually diving about here there and everywhere now it's so gentle. Is it by you Eric? (*Eric.* Yes.)

Ann. It might even touch you.

Eric. Wow! It's great that. *(as the trumpet touched him gently on the head.)*

We all chattered together on the trumpet's movements. At one point Jackie thought that the trumpet had gone far too high for the height of the ceiling, and we had to agree. With that the trumpet came back down as Stewart came out of trance and joined in the conversation.

Eric asked, "If when Dr Barnett said he would go to Jackie, did he mean through the trumpet?"

I told him. "No, no. He'll come out, materialise and walk across to her. He used to do that to Tom."

Stewart then asked where the trumpet was as he couldn't see the bright spots. It was up above head height near to June so out of his sight because of the cabinet curtain. Slowly it came back into view moving slowly out into the circle again. Ann asked him if he felt anything when it was moving slowly, as it was then, and he explained he only felt something when it touched anyone.

We then realised that the music had finished but the trumpet movement hadn't been affected as we had been constantly speaking.

Eric wanted to know who was controlling the trumpet.

June. Someone on the other side.

Eric. Yes but....

June. We don't actually know.

Stewart. We used to jest that it was Christopher, but I don't think it actually was Christopher. I don't think it is Walter either.

June. It's part of the 'team'. – It's team work isn't it?

Eric. Would this ever work in red light or does it have to be in complete darkness?

Stewart. But if you talk to me about that afterwards, Eric.

Eric. Okay.

Ann. In Tom's circle the trumpet was always in the dark.

Jane. There it goes again. (*as the trumpet took off from the table*)

June. It's had a rest. The team have had a tea-break. (*lots of laughter*)

Stewart. I wonder if we should sing just to lift the vibrations?

June. Do you want us to sing friends?

Jane started, "It's a long way to Tipperary" and we all joined in. This was followed by "Pack up your troubles." And then "I'm for ever blowing bubbles". With that the trumpet circled both ways and June welcomed Sunrise. Ann thought she heard a sound through the trumpet and shushed everyone.

Ann. Hush! Come on my love.

We then heard a strong "Woofff- woofff. ... We all here. ... Woofff- woofff"

Ann. Well done. You are all together.

Amidst all our comments his last words are lost but we heard the parting 'woofff', and the trumpet finally went down to the floor beside June. We then heard taps on the trumpet of Aye-tiddly-aye-tye followed by tye-tye on the table – probably with the drumsticks. (Perhaps indicating that Sam Hildred was there too.) Stewart went back into trance.

In a short time Freda was communicating and after a general chat for a few minutes she said "What I want is... I would like the lady Jackie to come and change places with you June. (*June.* No problem) I want to speak with you, dear. (*June.* Okay.)

Jackie moved across in the dim red light to June's chair beside Stewart and Ann guided June back to Jackie's chair.

Freda. Now give me your hand.

The light was then switched off.

Freda. Jackie, (*Jackie.* Yes) I wanted this opportunity to sit and hold your hand. I wanted to do that.

Jackie. – I'll listen to you. I know you are there for me.

There then came a husky breathing as someone else tried to come through. We eventually heard "Dad."

Jackie. Is that you Dad? (Yes....) Eric's here with me.

Eric. Hello.

Dad. I know, I know (*Jk.* Thank you for coming.) I know. I had to come, I had to come (*Jk.* I know you are looking after me.) Don't worry, don't worry (*Jk.* I won't. I know you're there.) Oh Yes.

Jackie. And do you like your little great granddaughter? Have you seen her?

Dad. What do you think! (*Jk.* Millie, she's lovely isn't she?) She's beautiful. (*Jk.* She is.) I will never get to meet her for many years but I will follow her with interest (*Jk.* I'm sure you will.) just as I'm with you. (*Jk.* Thank you.) This is so difficult for me. (*Jk & Eric.* You are doing very well.)... I am so thrilled to be here with you. (*Jk.* We are thrilled to have you here, Dad.)

Dad. Eric, Look after her. (*Eric.* I'll do my best.) Yes always, always. (*Jk.* Yes, yes.) I can't stay. ... (*Jk.* No, you've done very well, Dad. You've done very well, Thank you.) All my love, all my love....

Freda. Well, I think he did very well. You have a great closeness to your Papa. (*Jk.* I have.) I know, I know. (*Jk.* Yes very close.) I can always tell because a soul who is extremely close is always able to draw even closer and he has his right hand on your right shoulder as I speak. (*Jk.* Yes.) that is how close he is to you, dear. (*Jk.* Thank you.) Did he have tremors, dear? (*Jk.* Yes he had Parkinson's disease.) ... Yes. I thought so because I'm not certain if you noticed he was shaking all the time (*Jk.* Yes.) he was speaking and indeed it's on me now. I'm shaking myself.

Jackie. He was shaking a lot more than you are.

Freda. The reason for that is he is standing very, very close and I'm feeling this from him. I want you to know .... Who is Jim, dear .... do you know anything about a gymslip? (*Jk.* A gymslip? No.)... something to do with a gymslip (*June.* Well we all had them at school) Did you have them? (*addressing Jackie*)

Jackie. I must have done years ago. It was a long time ago – a long, long time ago.

Ann. Is it a memory from him?

Freda. Yes. I'm not certain – no matter no matter. They are all here and they are all wrapping you in love, dear. (*Jk.* Thank you, Freda.) Isn't that wonderful. (*Jk.* I'm very lucky.) ... Eric dear, you have a closeness with .... Just a moment, dear. Walter, just a moment I'm busy! (*June.* She doesn't change you know.) (*laughter from us*) ... Dr. Barnett wants to move on, dears. (*June.* Okay, okay.) This is important. (*June.* I know, I know.) This is more important than anything. Dr Barnett will try to do this something. Christopher may we have the light again, dear. (*Chris.* Are you ready for it now?) Yes. Now would you kindly remove the table from the circle and would you kindly remove the trumpet. You stay where you are dear.

June asked if they wanted the light out.

Freda. ... One moment I wonder ... Yes, Dr Barnett, just a moment. I wonder, Jackie dear, would you stand up. Would you take your chair and place it in the centre of the circle, and I want you to sit with your back to Stewart. (*Jk.* Right) ... That is fine, that is fine. Now Christopher you may switch off ... no, no, just a moment ... Ann, (*Ann.* Yes Freda.) I want you to do something dear. I want you to stand, take your chair, place it in front of Jackie so that you may sit facing her and I want you to take her hands, dear. (*Ann.* Okay.)

I moved across and sat as instructed, saying to Jackie 'Okay, just relax, just relax.'

Freda. Now, listen dears, I'm going to withdraw. Dr Barnett would like you all in a moment, once the light is extinguished – he would like you all to sing for a short time again to lift the vibrations. He will then attempt to materialise and then administer to you, Jackie dear. (*Jk.* Thank you.) All we ask of you is that you should relax, that is all – relax– close your eyes and relax. Now Christopher, would you switch off your light. Would you all now place your hands upon your knees with your palms uppermost. (*June.* We're ready Freda.) And now would you all kindly join together in song. (*Jane.* Okay. 'She'll be coming round the mountain'?) You may sing anything you wish (*June.* Okay Freda, thank you.) Once Dr Barnett has materialised ... once he begins to speak then would you all stop singing.

June. Yes.

We sang 'She'll be coming round the mountain' – all the verses for the next two minutes, when we heard Dr Barnett's hoarse breathing. I said "There's Dr Barnett. Oh! I can feel the cool air." Jane commented that it was lovely.

June. Well done, Dr Barnett.

Dr Barnett. Can you all hear my voice? (*Ann.* Very clear.) I shall reserve as much energy as I can for what I hope to do now. (*All.* Okay Dr Barnett / take our energy.) I shall speak a little later.

Dr Barnett. I bring now energy which I bring from my world. ... It is, as always, the weight which is so difficult for me to...

June. Has he got his hands on you, Jackie? (*Jk.* Yes.) .. just relax.

Dr Barnett. I merely want you to relax. That is all.

We heard long drawn out 'hollow' breaths, drawing in and pushing out the energy that he brought. This lasted for almost three minutes and then, as it went quiet, Dr Barnett spoke again "My dear,

I have done what I can. (*Jk.* Thank you, Dr Barnett.) All I ask now is that you allow me to come to you with the healing ministry by sending out your thoughts each evening. (*Jk.* I will.) Eric, I ask you, sir, again to do the same. *(Eric.* I will.) You are a dear soul – you are a dear soul. You are beloved of my world. Always remember that we are close by. (*Eric.* Yes. / *Jk.* Thank you.) Thank you for allowing me to work with you in this manner. (*Jk.* Thank you, very much / *E.* thank you for doing it.)

Dr Barnett. It is my pleasure, my pleasure, my privilege. God Bless you .... (*Several voices give their thanks.*) ... Stewart you must return to sleep .....

As all the energy had been used the circle was closed and we brought Stewart back out of trance.

What a wonderful evening it had been for our friends. It had taken us years to persuade Jackie – a vicar's daughter – it was "safe" to sit. For a number of years she was happy enough for Eric to receive healing, but she wouldn't remain in the room with us, even when we worked in their home, and sat in another room while he attended our Home Circle at Brayton, However, she had seen the good effect the healing work had done on Eric and was now able to benefit from it herself.

Unfortunately, although the healing could mollify the effects, the cancer was too far advanced and she passed peacefully into spirit two months later, at the beginning of June.

When I returned for Jackie's funeral, I was fortunate to be able to sit in the Hull Circle the following evening. As recorded in my book '*Harrison Connections*' Tom was the first to come through that evening to let us know all was well. Speaking through Stewart's trance but un-mistakably in his own voice:

Tom. You can hear? (*Everyone replies they can*) – It's hard. Trying so hard. It's Tom, Tom. Trying so hard to do this. Trying so hard to talk. Ann, darling, so pleased you're here.

Ann. I'm looking forward to this.

Tom. And me.

June. Steady as you go, Tom, steady as you go.

Tom. Don't know how much I shall be able to say. So Ann, Tell Eric ... (*Ann.* Yes. Tell Eric...) ... We've got her safe. (*Ann.* Yes.) She's here, ohhh, she's here. (*Ann.* That's great.) What a wonderful reunion. (*Ann.* Yes. I bet it was.) ... All here, all here. (*Ann.* With her mum and dad?) ... Make sure he knows that she ... all is fine, all is well, all is well!

Ann. He wants to know if you have been organising a party for her.

Tom. Well, I think you know the answer to that! (*Ann laughs –* Yes.) – Yes. Yes (*Ann.* He thought you would be.) ...What a wonderful, wonderful, wonderful time we have all had here since she came over (*nearly loses control*) (*Ann.* That's great.) No surprise to know I have been with you these past few ... (*Ann.* Days. Yes. No surprise.) ... Only wish that I could speak better than I am able to do at present, but it will come, it will come. (*Ann.* It will come. You are doing wonderful!) ... I thought that I would soon understand how to do this but it is far more difficult than even I could imagine it would be. ... We are having a wonderful time here. I know you will all understand if I don't speak to you all individually. How wonderful to be here again in this special place. Ohhh, ohhh, ohh (*very breathily - emotional*) special wonderful place. Ann, keep up all the good work. (*Ann.* Yes I'm trying to do that.) ... I feel exhausted now.

Ann. You must be. You've done so much. It's so hard. Well done.

Tom. I'll try again ... get the same old welcome, ohh, ohh... (*emotional*)

Tom. Ann, I said every night See you.. ohhh ... As I said every night... (*Ann.* Every night – 'Sleep tight'.) ... Sleep tight. I am with you.

(Tom used to say to me – 'Sleep tight...see you in the morning.')

Three months later I felt a strong impulse to sit with Stewart again, and they were happy to welcome me back again. It was to be a very special evening.

This is how I recorded it in *Harrison Connections*:

"At the start of the evening Tom spoke through Stewart, still concerned whether we could hear him:

Tom.. Can you hear?

Ann. Yes clearly. (*Katie*: Yes.) Even Katie can hear you.

(Katie is severely deaf but spirit have devised a method in the séance room by which she can hear.)

Tom. Well good old Katie!

Katie. Hello Tom, lovely to hear you again.

Tom. I … this is like old times. I know that … Ohh … I know what I want to say, but it's so hard – it's so very difficult to say a single word.

Ann. Well you are saying plenty of them. You are doing very well, Love.

Tom. Oh am I? (*June.* Yes. / *Carol.* Very clear, Tom.)... Ann, darling, I'm so happy that you are here. (*Ann.* Yes, so am I, so am I.) You know, people will not understand the difficult … the difficulty in saying what ... making myself understood ... so hard but I want you to know ... I want you all to know that all is fine here ... all is fine. I've met so many people ... Wonderful. I'm often with Gaynor, very often. I know that Cober is not far off. (*Ann.* That's right.) ... Be sure to give everyone my love.

A wonderful start to the night, back among such special friends. Katie Halliwell and I were sitting next to each other in the circle. We heard the sound of a materialised form moving out of the cabinet into the room, and shortly Katie announced that two hands were tapping on her head. At the same time the fingers of two hands were tapping, as though playing the piano, on my head. When I told everyone that I also had someone in front of me, Dr Barnett, to my right, said "Ann, my dear, there is no purpose in me spelling out to you whose hands they are."

For the 'experiment' that evening they had two people out of the cabinet, some 5-6 feet distance from the medium.

This was most unusual, and the second person was Tom. He played with my hair before slowly moving his hand to my shoulder, down my arm and tapping my knee. He then picked up my left hand

and cradling it between his two slim hands with their long fingers, I heard his familiar, emotional, "Ohh, ohh, ohh," as he tried to speak to me. But he could not control the energy needed to hold the form together and losing control of the ectoplasm it returned to the medium in the cabinet.

Instantly, I found larger hands were holding my outstretched hand. Hands I felt I recognised – Walter's hands.

As he took control, he spoke just one familiar word "Well." The fact that Walter was also out in the room amazed us.

June. Is that you, Walter?

Walter. It is folks.

June. Hello, Walter.

Walter. Ann, I want you to know this ma'am. That it would have been expecting rather too much for Tom to speak in addition to forming into materialisation, Okay. (*Ann*. He did very well.) – Folks, but I tell you this, that I would much rather speak through Stewart. It is darned difficult.

Dr Barnett. I would like to begin again.

Walter. Okay. Okay. Folks, I find this to be quite extraordinary. (*and he was gone*.)

Had we had three materialised forms, or part forms, there in the space in front of us?!

The experiment began again. Tom was not deterred, moments later he built again, and we could hear the effort it was for him to walk out of the cabinet.

He had always told us that spirit said carrying ectoplasm on their etheric bodies was like climbing out of a swimming pool in a sodden overcoat.

Knowing it was Tom, June told him not to try to move far, just speak.

Tom. Ann.

Ann. I know you are here, love. You are doing so well.

Tom. Wonderful. Oh, my love! (*Ann*. Yes, my darling.) ... If I say nothing else ... I... I want you to know this... that I am so settled, so settled. Miss you, miss you.

Ann. I miss you too.

Carol. We do miss you, Tom.

Tom. It's wonderful, wonderful. Ann, you know I'm often with you. (*Ann.* I know you are.) – Oh, Oh! (*emotionally*)

Ann. I think you did something special? (*I held a strong thought in my mind of my small crystal swan having been moved across the top of the bookcase.*)

Tom. Yes, yes! (Ann. That was a lovely surprise.)

And with a characteristic thump on the floor, as the ectoplasmic form collapsed – he was gone.

That was almost the end of the sitting for that evening but moments later, Walter returned to speak through Stewart's trance – which he had told us he preferred:

Walter. Folks we did our best. You know that for us, the process can be most frustrating. Those in ignorance of such matters may feel that the process should be simple. It is not, far from that. The fact that Tom was able to come to you, Ann – that in itself, is a virtual miracle. (*Ann.* Yes, I understand.) ... And I think that it demonstrates quite clearly the love that he has for you. (*Ann.* And me for him.) He made great efforts. Okay folks.

Just a few months after a medium friend had told me there would be a special occasion and I would feel him hold my hand – it had happened, just three days short of the eighteenth anniversary of our meeting. A very special 'anniversary' present!"

* * * * *

What news of Jackie?

Ten months after her passing it had been arranged for her husband and daughter Gill to sit at the circle but Eric did not feel well enough to attend that evening. Gill was given the full treatment of experiencing the matter-thru-matter experiment and was able to speak briefly to her mother with much encouragement and support by Freda.

Before Jackie came to speak, we heard this from Freda:

Freda. All I will say is this, you have heard various souls speaking this evening through the medium, understand that we have done so for many years, on a countless number of occasions we are what you might say is 'practised'– from a long association with the medium. Now for her to come and speak, it will be almost akin to her trying to move a mountain. So, all I can say is please do encourage her and I know she will do her best and no-one can do more than that, dear, no one. One moment, dear....

Within a few seconds, as we heard breathy sounds Gill encouraged her, "Mum are you coming through?"

Ann. Come on you can do this, love. We're all here for you.

Gill. You can do this. I know you want to...

We then heard, very quietly: "Oh.. oh ..oh yes, ..yes."

Gill. Mum, I know you're there.

Jackie. Yes. I'm here. I've been so worried... I've been so worried... I've been so worried ...This is wonderful, wonderful ... No more pain .... no pain.... Gill .... give everyone my love.

Gill. I will.

June. She's getting really excited, isn't she?

And with a gurgle she was gone.

We then heard another person trying to come through, a deeper male voice, Oh, oh, oh ,oh,

All. Nice 'n' steady – all right friend nice and steady.

A man's voice said – Arthur – Arthur. (*Ann.* Arthur?)[3]

"No! ... I want to speak with my Granddaughter."

Ann. You want to speak with your Granddaughter?

Gill. Grandpa?

Grandfather. Yes. Can you hear? (*This is a very strong voice.*)

Gill. I can hear.

Gr/f. I want to try to stay jolly close, to say that Mum's here. We're altogether here. We've tried very hard to reach him, you know. You know my thoughts about you (*Gill.* Yes. I do) Oh! Always mine, you were mine. You still are, never doubt it. I'm so proud of

---

3 The 'Arthur' had jumped in. It was a contact for me, from a neighbour, which Freda later gave me in full.

you. – I'll always be with you. (*Gill.* Thank you I know you are.) Not a day pa... I love you so much. (*Gill.* I love you too.)

And he was gone.

Within seconds Freda was back

Freda. Well I think that they both did remarkably well (*All comment of how well they did)* I think it shows such determination born out of considerable love. (*Gill.* Thank you.) Is there a dog here? Is there a dog? (*June.* In your world?) Yes, yes. Is there a connection here with a dog? Because your Grandfather is standing here and there's a dog running round in circles. (*Gill.* Bobby.) Yes. He's running round in circles. (*Gill.* Yes. He's their dog.) Yes, he's brought him with him. He's running round he's very excited, dear. (*Gill.* He was always very excited.) It's his dog. They are like two peas in a pod. (*Gill.* I hope he likes my dog now.) Oh, I'm sure that he does, dear.

A brief reunion but so very special.

It was a further 18 months before Eric was well enough (following a period in hospital) to attend the circle by which time the work had progressed.

Now the team were attempting to show transfigurations as well as trying to speak, but to do both was extraordinary. This was an evening when Eric and I were to be thoroughly 'spoiled'.

The communication that evening started with Freda asking me to sit beside Stewart so I could take his hand which helps with the contact. As I took his hand she said, "This is a hand that I remember very well indeed, dear. Now listen – it will not surprise you – it will not surprise any of you that your loved one is here (*Ann.* Yes.) this evening and I'm not speaking of Tom, though he is here, but Norman is here also. They are here together – here together.

Ann. That's what they tell me.

Freda. Yes. They are here together. ... He's trying to tell me something. I think the best thing I can do is to stand to one side so that he may come and speak.

We heard the familiar gurgling sounds of a voice trying to speak through Stewart's vocal chords.

Ann. Come on, Darling, you are doing so well.

Norman. Ann, my love, – Norm..

Ann. Yes, my love.

Norman I'm so pleased to be here speaking with you (*Ann.* It's lovely.)... Ann, just try to give me a few moments till I get used to speaking in this way. (*Ann.* Yes. you don't do it very often.) It's awfully difficult. I just wanted you to know I was close the other day when you fell and had a problem with your wrist. I told the lady to tell you so that you knew I was there. Ahhh....

Ann. Yes. That's good. It was silly the way I did it.

Norman. You know that Tom and I have met over here.

Ann. Yes I do. That is so good (*Norman.* Yes it is.) and you are busy working together?

Norman. Yes of course we are. We are doing all that we can. You know Ann, I'm so proud of the way that you have been able to go on. Now you are helping so many people. (*Ann.* I try.) Yes, yes, you are. Ann, Tom sends his love. (*sighing sounds as he can't hold on.*)

Ann. That's good. Well done, Darling, well done.

Freda returned "I think he did exceptionally well. (*Ann.* He did.)... Just a moment."

Another voice is very faintly heard trying to speak. As I was next to Stewart, I could hear that it was my mother.

Ann. That's lovely, come on.

Mum. At last, at last.

Ann. At last. Gosh you are doing so well. This is wonderful. What did you think to Isabel? Isn't she lovely with those dark eyes just like yours.

Mum. I'm trying so hard, but I just wanted you to hear my voice. (*And she was gone.*)

Ann. She was such a gentle person.

Carol. You can tell she was a gentle person.

Freda. Oh she tried so hard ... Who is Phil dear? (*Ann.* Phil?) Yes. (*Ann.* Oh, her friend – Phyllis) She's here. (*Ann.* Oh, they were such good friends.) Still are dear. They are together (*Ann.*

That's nice) ...they are together.... That's beautiful. ... Roaming in the gloaming ... What is this?

Ann. Gloaming that's dusk isn't it? ... in Scotland.

(As she said that, a picture flashed into my mind of an evening in Cornwall, many years before, when I was strolling with Norman along a lane beneath a double row of beech trees, with the bats happily insect hunting above us – definitely in the 'gloaming'. A lovely memory.)

Freda. This is something of significance . ... Raymond in a few moments we shall call for the light. Now, Ann dear, *(Ann.* Yes.) when we require the light to be extinguished I shall do this *(she made a movement (squeeze) with her hand – Stewart's hand)* and then you give the instruction to Raymond switch off the light. We would like to try an experiment All we ask my dears is that you should look in this direction *(towards Stewart)* and we shall do our best... When we require the light on we do that, Ann. *(a different signal was given to my hand)* and off we do that. *(Ann.* Okay. Yes.) I shall return shortly, dears. Again, as Walter says, if you are able to see anything we need to hear ... we need to know it is important. We do not always know ourselves if we are meeting with success.

Ray. Okay Freda?

Freda. Yes I shall return shortly, dears. .....

After a short time Carol spoke. "There's a lot of facial changes, a lot of movement ... his face looks completely different from here *(to left of Stewart)* I don't know what it's like from your side. I don't know what anyone else thinks.

Ann. It's just in shadow at my side.

Carol. Right. It's quite clear this side. I can see features quite well.

There are sounds of raspy breathing and then the signal to turn the light off. We heard a voice and Freda spoke: "On the next occasion Raymond you may switch the light up. *(Ray.* Turn it a bit higher?) Yes turn it a bit higher. *(Ray.* Okay) Not now.

Ray. I know – when you are ready. I understand.

Freda. I know a great deal depends on where you happen to be sitting."

Ann. Yes I do know. It was just at my side I could see a profile, but it was all in shadow.

Freda. Yes that's why we require the light to be switched up a little. ... We shall try again ... Lisa, Jane we want you to look also. If you see anything we need to know. We need your guidance, dears.

Some seconds passed before I got the signal and said "On."

Lisa and Carol were sitting more full on, said they could see a shape forming.

Chris commented that there was like a big white beard.

Ray. Down his front, it's all the energy isn't it?

Carol. Yes, where it's all moving about. I can see the spirit eyes now. The energy they are putting into it, in shaping the eyes! (*Jane.* Is the face broader?) It's definitely changed. The eyes from here are looking ..

Ray. They looking around

Ann. There was a flash of light across the cheekbone then.

Carol. Is this forming into Tom?

Ann. Oh! It is!

Carol. It's Tom!

Ann. Darling, it's wonderful. I can see the nose, the length of the face. Wonderful, Brilliant!

Carol.. Very distinctive

*Ann.*Well done, well done. That's lovely.

Carol. That's absolutely amazing! Trying to talk to us. (there were a few sounds of someone trying to speak, we heard −"Ohh, ohhh."

Ann. Darling, that's brilliant.!

Tom. (*breathily*) Ohh, ohhh, Yes, yes.

Ann. A different shape from Stewart's.

Carol. Very much so.

With a big sigh the image faded − and I had the signal for the light to be turned off.

Carol. That was fantastic /*Ann.* That was amazing!

Carol. It all came together into his face and you could see it quite distinctly.

Freda. This is what we are trying so hard to do, dears, and if you are able to see your loved ones even for a few moments that makes our task worthwhile.

Ann. And with that just bit brighter light as well, it made it so much easier. That was wonderful.

Freda. Well ... we are encouraged ourselves. (*almost shouting with excitement*)

Everyone joined in saying how wonderful, then Freda added – "Well as we always say, Lisa dear we are never certain ourselves whether we are meeting with success and that is precisely why we need guidance from yourselves, but your dear one, Tom – our dear one, Tom, tried so hard to show himself ...(*Ann.* He did, he did.) Oh I feel so.. elated!

Carol. We do too. It all came together and I could see him clear as a bell.

Freda. So isn't that wonderful.

Freda then returned to give me more from my mother. She had passed in 1976, so a long time in our years and although I had heard from her once through Glynn Edwards, the wonderful trance/mental medium, I had never heard from her in a physical séance. Because she was in life a gently determined, quiet lady I know to impinge her thoughts on to a male medium must have taken a great effort. However, Freda was able to give me some wonderful memories as well as a very recent happening.

Freda. Your mother wants you to know dear that although she rarely communicates, it's taken a long, long time but she wants you to know that she is here this evening and she is insistent that I pass her love over to you. She's such a gentle soul. ... Is it you who likes liver or was it her?

Ann We all used to. (*Freda.* She cooks liver.) Yes, she did nearly every week I think – liver and onions. (*Chris* – 'n gravy!) Yesss! (*Carol.*– Mashed potato!) Yesss!

Freda. She loved tulips too.

Ann. She did we had a garden full of tulips.

204

Freda. She's saying I have to mention the tulips. (*Ann.* Yes.) These are memories that I'm bringing back to you. ...

Ann. That's very special, yes. Along the little path down to the wash-house.

Freda. May I ask, dear, did you when you were a small child wear a bow on top of your head (*Ann.* Yes) because she's showing me this picture of a little girl that must be you with a bow on top of the hair.

This was the photo I was looking at a few days earlier. Taken by photographer Sandy Lewis in the '40s, so my father had photos of us to take to war with him.

Ann. I was looking at it the other day at her grand-daughter's.

Freda. That is to say – You see how clever they are because they want you to know that they are always around. She saw that dear, she saw that.

Ann. Good, good, because I was with her Great-granddaughter.

Freda followed this with – "Is it you that likes cinder toffee dear? (*Ann.* Yes.) I feel silly mentioning something like that... (*Ann.* Tom's mum made cinder toffee.) I see, I see, but all these people are here tonight for you. Isn't that wonderful. ... Raymond, the light, dear. Ann will you kindly return to your seat and take your loved ones ... (*Ann.* ...take them with me....(*smiling*)) They will always be with you, looking over your shoulder, dear.

Freda then asked Eric to sit with her and to imagine he was holding 'her' hand and not a male hand (Stewart's). Freda chatted with Eric for quite some time, passing on love to their daughters, and telling Eric that Jackie was often with him in sleep state, though he wouldn't remember. Then Carol was given instructions about the switching on and off of the light as they wanted to do anther experiment.

After some half minute we heard Carol say 'Light, Ray.'

Carol. Stewart's features have gone. I can't see any at all.

Jane. Last time it really looked like a piece of material over his head, it's all bubbly this time.

Carol. Yes. The hair has definitely changed hasn't it. There's hair there. (*Jane.* Yes) Come on then, you can do it. Got to hear you voice, Eric, then she.... (*Ann.* Come on then!)

Eric. Come on, keep trying, you're doing very well.

Jane. I keep thinking I see marcel waves, you know how they did tight waves from the 20s.

Carol. Yes the hair style, Definitely.

Eric. Keep trying you are doing very well.

Carol. The hair is amazing really taking shape now.

We hear breathy breathing then the Voice says – "Can you hear, hear? It's Jackie. It's me, it's me."

Eric. Hello, ... hello Jack.

Jackie. Ohh , ohh!

Ann. All right, darling, don't get too excited.

Carol. Jackie. Ohhh.

Eric. Don't get upset. It's lovely to hear you.

As we tried to calm her she was unable to control it and with a gulp (*on Stewart's voice*) she left. Carol got the signal to extinguish the light.

Once the light was extinguished we heard Stewart's voice being controlled and she returned. "It's Jack, Jackie (*Eric.* I'm still here.) It's Jackie ... Jackie ... (*Eric.* Hello Jack. It's lovely to hear you.) ... I was so worried, so worried... I wished so I could see you again, so long ... so hard. Oh, ohh."– in a rasping breath and as we heard a creak of Stewart's chair she was gone.

She was a very strong character.

Freda then – (*as she had with me*)– passed on personal messages from Jackie – reminiscences. Closing with – "Oh, I wish that I could do much better but you know, my dears, it is so difficult being between the two worlds – I'm listening to you – I'm listening to them."

Eric. Yes, yes but you've been able to convey Jackie's love to me and mine to her. That's what it's all about and I'm absolutely delighted.

Freda. All you ever need to do, dear, is to send out a thought and she is aware. She catches your thoughts. If you ever to be with her, send out thoughts before you sleep. I know that you have done this. Send out thoughts to her before you sleep and she will be able to join you.

Eric. Ohh ! that's lovely!

* * * * *

Such very special reunions,

Jackie with her Dad, and then, after her passing, with her daughter and her husband;

For Gill with her mother and her Grandfather – and his dog;

For me to hear my mother after thirty-seven years and have it confirmed she was with me when I held her Great-granddaughter, and Norman, my first husband, who had been in spirit for twenty-three years, but was still watching over me when I had a fall;

And to see Tom show himself by transfiguration, and hear him, albeit briefly, just three years after his passing.

This was a never to be forgotten series of sittings.

Thank you, Stewart, and your dedicated sitters and the Spirit Team.

As I started this chapter, I heard that Eric had passed into spirit himself, at the beginning of March 2023. So, ten years after speaking to his wife they will now be reunited with the great love that they had for each other.

In Closing

I have many more accounts of physical mediumship and their phenomena that I could go on for pages and pages, but they would pale into insignificance after these I have selected.

Nor does it always have to be in the séance room. We had it happening several times with apports, particlularly of coins appearing in unusual places. For us the spirit folk would show their presence by the projector changing 'slides' automatically when at talks or even before talks when no -one was touching it or even holding the slide changer control. (The control was plugged into the back of the projector but you were able to use it at some distance.)

The first time it occurred was in May 1996 at Billingham church, with Ann Robson, a powerful trance medium. I had set up the projector and adjusted the focus for sharpness when, with no one touching it, the slide changer moved and changed the slide. I was by the projector and Tom and Ann were some distance away talking. I did not have the control in my hand and there was no earthly reason for the slide to have changed.

In London, November 1996, at the end of the talk for SPR members Tom was answering questions when suddenly the slide changed. I was sitting behind the projector but I had put the control down, as we did not contemplate having to change any again. There were, however, members of a physical circle sitting just one row back from me, and they had lost one of their members very recently. Margarete told me later that she has asked him to show them he was present. Could that have been the sign? She certainly thought it was.

One hot evening in Louth, Lincolnshire, (1999) Tom asked me if it was cool enough to turn the projector off so he didn't have to speak over the fan. It seemed not, as suddenly the slide changed without touching it. It caused quite some amusement. (*Saying keep going!?*)

In June 1999 we were up at South Shields. At the end of my talk on the work of Billy Hope, I was showing the Frank Leah drawing of Billy Hope. I left it on the screen and had placed the slide changer on the lectern. I picked up the torch pointer to point at a part of the drawing when suddenly the projector back tracked to the picture before. Someone was demonstrating they were present.

Although we continued to use this projector and its multichange carrier until 2008, when we changed to a digital projector and Power Point presentations, we never had these happenings again. It seems there was no familiar physical object for them to "play with" and to let us know of their presence with us.

On quite a different note, years later, in 2011, when it appeared that Tom was attempting EVP, he had told me 'only give me time'. Two years later he did it, albeit briefly. Unfortunately, I didn't find what he had achieved for some time. Six years later, when listening to a recording of my Sunday morning Address in the service at the Acacia Centre in 2013, I heard his voice echoing mine with the word "enjoying" — not quite overlapping, but clearly there. It was definitely his voice, demonstrating without a doubt, that they are always by you in support and love.

The main point to convey in all of this is the overwhelming love that is brought from those who return, whether they are your loved ones returning, entertainers or great teachers. As one sitter said, after the first time he sat in the circle in Spain, "I felt very nervous before we started but once that energy built up, it made you feel you couldn't be frightened of anything."

For physical phenomena to happen so much must take place within a safe home circle situation. For the very best to be possible – for materialisation to happen – the energy constituents need to be familiar and contstant. In a public gathering it is much more difficult. It is like a making a cake – add different ingredients or quantities to a reliable 'known' recipe and you may have an inedible result. The energies and emotions of so many are not known before-hand when the team starts to make their preparations. This is why so many times what they do appears to be repetitive – 'Party tricks' to placate the sitters, but the team knows they can get a result and keep them happy. If the honest seeker / investigator would take away the impulse – the thrill – provided by the public gathering and sit in harmony with friends or family, at home, who knows what time might bring.

No time is ever wasted. If you gain nothing you have provided energy for your friends in spirit to work with, in a direction where it is needed – and who knows what you may also be learning, subliminally.

The phenomena which I have recounted here demonstrates that there is life – there is consciousness – beyond this world which we consider 'solid', that is trying to show us that there is more. This 'solid' world can be manipulated by them to bring our attention to this fact. They use this facility to gain our attention to the fact that there is so much more for us to learn.

We are all Spirit. It is the life force that makes life here possible, but we are also a soul—the consciousness that drives our life—that tries to prompt us to do things—to follow a path to greater knowledge and spiritual understanding of loving kindness.

Many years ago, the wonderful mediums Alec and Louie Harris had a guide called White Wing. ...

... and White Wing said, "The Phenomena of what you call Spiritualism is the Door; the Philosophy is the Hall, but we want you to come into the Dining Room and partake of the food the Great White Spirit has prepared for you. So many are content to remain at the Door. The Master Jesus attracted multitudes by performing miracles but when they were gathered together, he preached to them of Spirit. We come to demonstrate phenomena, but we expect you to search and learn more of the Great White Spirit."

They have opened the door for me, and I hope I have now opened the door for you, and although you may not experience what I have, you may decide to enter and "partake of the food the Great White Spirit has prepared for you." Whether it be starting your own home circle, or healing, supporting and giving – living with loving kindness – do it with all your heart, and may you find your path and follow it with joy.

Give it your all –and have no regrets.

Milton Keynes UK
Ingram Content Group UK Ltd.
UKHW020741080324
438959UK00014B/548